SOFT SKILLS

"Your Key to a Better Job & Higher Pay!"

By John Eric Jacobsen

Copr. JBP, Inc., 2021 – JohnEricJacobsen.net

Dedication

I dedicate this book to all of the wonderful people I've met in my seminars and workshops nationwide who were struggling to pay bills, stressed to be unemployed, unhappy in a job, or worried about finding a job. I hope I was able to help you release those pressures and reach your goals.

Special Thanks

I'm sending out a very special thanks to all of my dear family, friends, and colleagues who supported me through this book. They inspired me and made everything possible: The Folks, Kathy, Erica, Jessica, Mark, Deb, JG, AG, Richy, Vincenza, Carla, Sophia, Dez, Gen, Isaias, Jackie Jenkins. Thanks to all of my teachers, trainers, authors, motivators, and mentors from whom I've amassed the following 30 years of information and insights: James Needham, Brian Tracy, Helen Francis, Ken Coscia, Milton Trachtenburg, Fred Pryor, Jose Silva, K. Paul Grivas, June Graham, Ron G - Thank You!

Very Special Note

This book is written in a conversational style and formatted in an instructional fashion. Much of the information is drawn from my live seminars or training.

A small portion of this book contains some updated material from my 2013 release "Weapons of Mass Instruction."

John Eric Jacobsen

Jacobsen Business Seminars, Inc.

Copyright, 2021 JBP, Inc.

JohnEricJacobsen.net

It is unlawful to reprint, republish, or redistribute any part of this book in part or in full without written permission from the author and publisher.

Great Feedback

"I have been unsuccessfully looking for work and applying for jobs for over two years. The Soft Skills book helped me to clean up my resume and improve my interviewing skills. I am now working at a wonderful job with an excellent salary and benefits. Mr. Jacobsen's book has been a life-saver for me, and I wholeheartedly recommend it. I believe that Mr. Jacobsen's book will be around long after the others are gone."–Ms. Jean Marie Lowens Manchester, NH

"What a great and necessary book for job seekers. This book has many soft skill strategies for anyone looking to develop their interpersonal and people skills. It is excellent and straightforward to read. I recommend it to all of my clients." – Ms. Kathy Parrin, NFL Films

'I read this book while preparing for an interview for a better job. It strengthened my confidence, and I landed the job based on the communication principles I applied from this book. I recommend this book to everyone wanting to find a better job. Soft Skills is a "Must-Read!" – Mr. John Gigante, Westchester, NY

"Without a doubt, a must-read book for any business professional looking to develop their soft skills. I recommend reading it with a highlighter." – Ms. Gen Kacmarcik, Rutherford, NJ

"Three weeks after reading the Soft Skills book, I started my own recording business. The book taught me to improve my people skills and my communication skills. I was very impressed with the information on body language and how it can influence my customers and sales. Mr. Jacobsen, thank you for this book and the hidden confidence it helped me find. – Ms. Lori Lagomarsini, Tampa, Florida

"This is the best and most informative book about Soft Skills I have ever read. The information about making a great first impression and how to professionally recover from a blunder is fascinating. I also used the communication tools to negotiate a better salary. I highly recommend this book! – Ms. Jaime Light, Staten Island, NY

Soft Skills
Table of Contents

A Quick Introduction!	Page - 5
Chapter 1 - What are "Soft Skills?"	Page - 7
Chapter 2 - Land Your Dream Job by Properly Setting Your Goals	Page -10
Chapter 3 - Rapport is Power!	Page -17
Chapter 4 - Soft Skills and a Positive Attitude	Page -28
Chapter 5 - Soft Skills and Communication Mastery	Page -39
Chapter 6 - Soft Skills and Assertiveness	Page -56
Chapter 7 - Applying Soft Skills to Negative People	Page -62
Chapter 8 - Soft Skills and Customer Service	Page -71
Chapter 9 - Soft Skills and Telephone Mastery	Page -108
Chapter 10 - Soft Skills and Dealing with Conflict	Page -120
Chapter 11 - Mastering Your Time & Enhancing Your Productivity	Page -136
Chapter 12 - HOT Networking Tips	Page -143
Chapter 13 - The Anatomy of a Job Interview	Page -147
Chapter 14 – How to Write a Great "Thank You" Email	Page -157
Chapter 15 – Soft Skills and Answering Tough Interview Questions	Page -163
Chapter 16 – Commit to Being a Life-Long Learner	Page -172
Chapter 17 – Soft Skill Strategies for Accelerating Your Career	Page -178
Ye Olde Office Rules	Page -181
About the Author!	Page -182

A **Quick** Introduction

CONGRATULATIONS! By reading this book, you've made a significant investment in your career and earning potential whether you're looking for a new job or changing careers. Or, perhaps you're already employed and want to accelerate your career. Or, maybe you're a CEO or manager interested in teaching these valuable soft skills to your team. This book and the information it contains will be your priceless resource for years to come.

The information contained in this book will show you how to improve your market value and your hire-ability factor. You'll master superstar employability skills to skyrocket your communication style, develop your charisma, resolve conflict, deal with negativity, improve your customer service, master your time, improve your productivity, and cultivate a healthy, contagious personality. With these invaluable soft skills under your belt, you'll be on the fast track to a more fulfilling, higher-paying career.

I've witnessed this book help people of all ages find meaningful jobs, accelerate their careers, and rapidly put the pieces of their lives back together.

Developing your soft skills will have a significant impact on your life and career.

Before we begin our soft skills journey, I find it necessary to describe my intent and sole-purpose for putting this book together.

My Five Objectives Are:

1. To provide you with practical, usable information designed to help you land your dream job.

2. Help you master the essential soft skills that head hunters, prospectors, and hiring managers hold in high demand.

3. To help you attain higher than expected earnings.

4. To help you accelerate your career.

5. To provide information you can share with your teams for increasing camaraderie and productivity.

Every word, example, story, and anecdote in this book focuses on helping you realize the above outcomes. Your success will make all of these efforts worthwhile for me.

I know you'll find great benefit in these pages, and as always, I wish you luck and success.

John Eric Jacobsen Marlton, NJ January 2021

Chapter 1

What Are Soft Skills?

Employers throughout our country are looking for two types of skills: Hard Skills & Soft Skills.

Hard Skills are also known as "technical skills." They are teachable skills that can be measured when applied. These may include but are not limited to computer skills, designing software, formatting, reading, writing, accounting, typing speed, language proficiencies, and operating machinery.

On the other hand, **Soft Skills** are "people skills" or "employability skills." These skills make you a valuable employee. Some examples include being a great communicator, possessing excellent listening skills, charisma, a pleasing personality, a positive attitude, leadership qualities, problem-solving abilities, conflict resolution, and the ability to get along with lots of different types of people.

Prominent companies such as Disney, Virgin Atlantic, Ritz-Carlton, Harley Davidson, and numerous others maintain that during their hiring process, they are not only looking for competent candidates but, more importantly, they're seeking happy, positive candidates. Why?

"Did you know that corporate America spends over 3 billion dollars per year dealing with negativity and difficult employees in the workplace?"

The new corporate mindset is to conserve that money by hiring positive people with developed soft skills in the first place. The belief is that this new, selective hiring will help combat negativity, decrease stress, and reduce the turnover rate, thereby improving corporate culture.

Over 75% of hiring managers and Human Resource Associates report that interpersonal or people skills are more important than technical skills. Many leaders are more interested in hiring a candidate with impeccable character and teaching them technical skills after hiring. The International Association of Administrative Professionals, OfficeTeam and HR.com, state that 67% of HR managers said they'd hire a candidate with strong soft skills even if his or her technical abilities were lacking. It should also be no surprise that more than 33% of job candidates with inadequate soft skills receive a rejection notice after their interview.

Now, before we go any further, let me be clear that I am in **no way** knocking, bashing, or disregarding hard, technical skills. They are essential in almost every job or career choice.

"The ideal candidate is proficient in both hard and soft skills."

I am saying that it is easier and more time-effective for a hiring manager or team leader to train technical skills than to educate and develop soft skills in an employee.

It doesn't matter how knowledgeable you are or how many degrees you've achieved; if you don't know how to smile, create rapport, and help a customer feel comfortable, your chances of being hired significantly diminish. It doesn't matter if you are a computer and a mathematical genius; if you can't get along with your co-workers and team members, they will fire you. Your "market-value" as a candidate is bleak if you are a product knowledge mastermind yet, you lack the communication skills, finesse, clarity, and personality to present that information to clients. The fact is **Soft Skills** rule!

At the end of this book, you will be better able to:

1. Better understand the importance of soft skills, interpersonal skills, and building partnerships with others.

2. Better understand the importance of practical communication skills.

3. Utilize the required tools to be prepared and competitive in today's workplace, therefore, increasing your market value.

4. Understand the importance of working well and effectively with team members or co-workers.

5. Learn and apply the soft skills required by employers to help you to be successful on the job.

6. Think creatively and be a contributing member of a problem-solving team.

7. Create a plan for your job search, including resume, cover letter, and developing your interview skills.

8. Enhance your employment presentation skills to assist you in achieving your career goals.

Chapter 2

Landing Your Dream Job by Properly Setting Your Goals

The first step toward landing your dream job to have a concrete goal. You must have a firm image in your mind of the exact type of job or career you desire. You must make this decision before you begin your job search. If you haphazardly begin looking for a job without a plan, you'll end up taking the first job offered to you and be very unhappy. You must specifically know:

1. What is the ideal job or career you desire, best matching your skills and talents?

2. What type of salary range will be satisfactory for you?

3. What kind of healthcare or medical benefits are required?

4. How far are you willing to travel?

5. What company or industry would you find exciting?

6. What did you like/dislike about your previous job?

7. What things do you do best?

"Remember, hazy goals produce hazy results and will create a less than satisfactory outcome. 63% of Americans hate their jobs, and you do not want to be one of them."

Human beings are "goal-seeking mechanisms." The excitement that pumps through your body when you are pursuing a worthwhile goal is exhilarating. That powerful energy keeps you alive and feeling passionate. As human beings, our happiness is magnified when we are working towards the fulfillment of our desires. Goals are vitamins for your soul. It does not matter how small or large your goals are or the type of career you're pursuing. By applying the following 6-step formula, you will be better focused and prepared to begin your job search. On a personal note, I have used the following method throughout my adult life, and it has helped me achieve many great successes on many different levels. I'm sure it will help you, too.

The 6 Step Goal Achievement Formula

1. You Must Know What You Want!

I have already mentioned this point, and it is a significant step in goal setting. You must know what you want, and you must write it down. You must also be able to state your goal in one short sentence or less. If you cannot speak your goal in one short sentence or less, you do not have clear, concise goals. If your goals are not specific, you will design a hazy, sloppy future condemning yourself to a life of mediocrity. You cannot reach your goals unless you know what they are. You must aim your mind at specific targets.

What specific outcomes do you desire? What end result do you have in mind? One of the most popular weekend vacations is the famous "Cruise to Nowhere." This popular cruise has a very specific destination. The passengers realize that they are going to "nowhere," and then they'll return. I'm sure you'll agree; even "nowhere" is "somewhere" if that is where you're aiming. Knowing this, you must direct your mind to a specific target before you can hit the bull's eye.

Distinctively, write out all of your goals in a personal notebook and review them regularly. For each of your goals, list at least ten benefits you will receive when you achieve that goal. Review these benefits for several minutes in the morning and several minutes before retiring. You will then be pounding these benefits into your subconscious mind giving you the momentum to persist. Remember, a goal correctly set is halfway attained.

Here are some examples:

"I am now happily employed as a customer service rep earning over $50,000 per year.

"I am now happily employed as a coach, working close to home with flexible hours, earning over $100,000 per year."

"I am now happily living my life's dream as an accountant. I own and operate my business earning over $250,000 per year."

2. Design a Flexible Plan and Follow It.

Once you have a specific goal, job, or career in mind, your next step is to draw up a plan to achieve it. The dictionary defines the word "plan" as a systematic method for accomplishing something. Planning is a tool that can help us to reach our goals. It is the vehicle that transports us from where we are to where we want to be. A good plan will keep you on course and shorten the road to your goal. I have made many mistakes in my life by not creating practical plans. I was under the impression that I just needed to have a goal, and then everything else would effortlessly fall into place. I fooled myself. Having a plan is a tool that will dramatically improve your goal achievement success rate.

Follow your plan precisely the way you designed it. If, during your journey, you decide to alter your plan, then do so. Flexibility is a key to success. Begin working steadily toward your dreams; you'll be amazed how fast your ship will come in if you swim out to meet it with a plan.

Here are some things to begin planning:

      A. Begin designing your cover letter and resume.

      B. Get your online profiles set up. (Specifically, LinkedIn)

      C. Learn how to answer tough interview questions.

      D. Decide the time of day you will begin online research.

      E. Create a schedule indicating how long you'll research.

3. Identify Any Obstacles and How to Avoid Them.

By identifying any obstacles you may encounter on your job search, you will be better prepared to avoid them. Statistically, there are many bumps and potholes on the road to employment. But, if you've prepared yourself with tools and mental agility, you will land your job unscathed.

Once you identify any obstacles, reach out to people who can assist you in overcoming those obstacles. Perhaps they are people who have faced the same challenges and successfully circumvented them. Ask if they'd like to be your mentor. Possibly, you can utilize some online connections. Consistently ask for advice, read job search articles online, read books, and watch interview videos. Always remember the **6 Ps** of job searching.

P – roper

P – rior

P – lanning

P – revents

P – oor

P - erformance

Here are some obstacles you may encounter:

    A. Do you need to attend any classes to further your education?

    B. Must you learn some new computer programs?

    C. Have you rehearsed your phone interview skills?

    D. Do you need a diploma, or will your skills alone be sufficient?

    E. Are your typing skills up to par?

    F. Do you have a quiet place to do your research?

    G. Do you need to make any arrangements for your family or children?

4. Use Positive Affirmations Daily for Reinforcement Purposes.

Affirmations and positive self-talk are popular techniques used for programming your subconscious mind. They are potent tools that can keep your momentum, spirits & enthusiasm high on your job search. It can be rough out there, and positive affirmations are a helpful and healthful remedy to help you remain focused. Your affirmations must be clear, concise, positive suggestions designed to influence your subconscious and motivate you to reach your goals.

Here are some great examples:

"I can do it!"

"I'm heading for something bigger and better sooner than I think."

"I'm on my way to a fulfilling career."

"Every day as days go by, my confidence levels increase."

"I got this!"

"I deserve a better, higher-paying career."

5. Keep Your Goals a Secret & Avoid Vampires!

The easiest person to find on this Earth is someone who will tell you, *"You won't succeed," "It can't be done," or "I tried that, and it didn't work."* Anyone who discourages you from your dreams is called a "vampire." These people suck the energy out of you by shedding negativity on your goals. You'll be surprised how many people will be threatened by your success. It is written in the New Testament to *"Go forth and tell no one,"* and *"Do not tell your left hand what your right hand does."* Whatever your religious beliefs, the wisdom in these writings teaches us to **SHUT UP!** Keep your dreams and goals a secret. Do not tell anyone what lies ahead in your future unless you know they will support your efforts. Don't tell anyone you're seeking a better job or a more lucrative career. Envy does strange things to people, and their negativity will sour your spirits. Sadly, as you climb the ladder of excellence, you will discover who your real friends are. Share your dreams and goals only with like-minded people who will support and assist you. These people are success-minded, and they will hold the ladder of success steady for you as you climb.

Surround yourself only with winners. Be like the customer who went into the restaurant and ordered lobster. When the waiter delivered the lobster to the table, the customer noticed that the lobster's front claw was missing. The customer asked, *"What happened to this lobster's front claw?"* The waiter responded, *"He lost it in a fight."* The customer demanded, *"Bring me the winner! I'll only eat the winner!"*

Emulate this customer and associate only with the winners. Keep your goals and career aspirations a secret. It is easier to find work when you have positive support from others. As for the negative vampires, let them see your dreams after they materialize, not before. I find it very interesting that recently, the world is so highly interested in vampire movies and TV shows. Perhaps it's because it's something we subconsciously recognize about ourselves or others. Remember, you never rise higher than the people with whom you associate.

6. Persist, Persist & Never Give Up!

Research states that, on average, you'll need to have five in-person interviews before you land your job. Statistically, you'll need to knock on several doors before the right job answers. When you have faith and a positive mental attitude, you realize that a so-called "failure" is only a different result or a "delayed success." Failure is a precious lesson teaching us to try another road. Failure allows us to alter our plans and to discover a better way. High achievers profit from their mistakes. When you study successful people's lives, you will learn they have dozens of failures in their portfolio. That would put us in good company. People on the road to excellence expect occasional setbacks, yet they always pick themselves up --- persist and keep dancing.

Persistence will make you a winner. Perseverance will give you the power to hold on when the road is rough, the ability to meet every obstacle, smile, and move on. Usually, when defeat overtakes a person, they will quickly retreat. That is one of the reasons the bottom of the success ladder is very crowded. Success only releases its rewards and shines its beautiful face when a person refuses to quit. You must be willing to gamble all that you have to get through the door leading to victory. Persistence helps you stack the odds in your favor. As you journey toward the realization of your dreams, make failure your teacher, not your undertaker.

Remember: If you plan to be an "overnight success," I guarantee that you'll be destroyed by morning. You will not have earned the "resiliency" or the "staying power" that winners have developed by being lucky enough to fail.

Once, an older man was financially broke, living in a tiny house, and owned a beat-up car. He was living off of $99 social security checks. At 65 years of age, he decided things had to change. So he thought about what he had to offer. His family and friends raved about his chicken recipe. He agreed that this was his best shot at making a change.

He left Kentucky and traveled to different states trying to sell his recipe. He told restaurant owners that he had a mouthwatering chicken recipe. He offered the recipe to them for free, just asking for a small percentage of the items sold. It sounds like a good deal, right?

Unfortunately, most of the restaurants did not agree. The man heard "NO" over 1000 times. Even after all of those rejections, he didn't give up. He believed his chicken recipe was something special. He got rejected 1009 times before he heard his first "yes!"

With that one success, Colonel Hartland Sanders changed the way Americans eat chicken. Kentucky Fried Chicken, popularly known as KFC, was born.

Remember, never give up and always believe in yourself despite the rejections you may face as a job seeker. I promise you're heading for something bigger and better sooner than you think.

Chapter 2 Review

1. You must know what you want with a definite purpose.

2. Design a flexible plan and implement it.

3. Identify and clarify any obstacles and how to avoid them.

4. Use passionate affirmations to keep you motivated.

5. Keep your goals a secret and avoid vampires.

6. Persist and never give up!

7. View perceived failures as gifts and opportunities.

8. Land your dream job!

Chapter 3

Rapport is Power!

The most important key to superior soft skills is the ability to build rapport with people. You build or create rapport when you develop mutual trust, friendship, and affinity with someone. Building rapport can be extremely advantageous to your career. It can help you to establish good interpersonal relationships, and this will open many doors for you. You cannot succeed in your career or any area without rapport. Rapport is also an essential ingredient for building trust and credibility at your job interview. Amazingly, the sole-purpose of soft skills is to help you build rapport with others. Rapport gives you the power and the upper hand in every situation. What is rapport?

"Rapport is a close and harmonious relationship in which the people or groups understand each other's feelings or ideas and communicate well."

There are two types of rapport: "Light Rapport" and "Deep Rapport."

Light Rapport is created during a first impression, such as meeting someone for the first time. Light rapport means the other person "likes" you and thinks you're "nice." They may be impressed by how you look, present yourself, or your personality. It is an essential type of rapport but not important enough to land a job, especially a high paying job.

Deep Rapport happens at a profound subconscious level. Deep rapport signifies the other person not only likes you; they also "trust" you. If your soft skills and communication expertise are underdeveloped, it may take weeks, months, or years to gain trust from another person. Trust must be earned. Yet if you are an excellent communicator, trust and deep rapport can be acquired relatively quickly. For your success, you must achieve a deep rapport with the hiring manager at your first interview. Remember, it's essential that they "like" you, but if they don't "trust" you, they'll never hire you.

The Top 5 Essential Soft Skills for Creating Rapport

1. Making a Great 1st & 2nd Impression.

2. Body Language.

3. Non-Verbal Communication.

4. The Handshake.

5. Eye Contact.

Making a Great 1st & 2nd Impression at Your Interview

Did you know some research indicates that it takes only 15 seconds in a face to face interview for the hiring manager to form a solid first impression about you? Imagine that! You have just fifteen seconds to persuade that manager to hire you. That's a lot of pressure to deal with on your part. It's almost as if they carry an imaginary report card and mentally score everything they like or dislike you.

Professor Albert Mehrabian has pioneered a profound understanding of communication skills and established many new concepts revolving around the art of body language. The following is a more common and over-simplified interpretation of Mehrabian's findings. Yet, it's enough to serve the soft skill agenda of this book.

During the first 15 seconds of the first impression, the hiring manager makes several judgments about you.

55% of the first impression (which is over half) is a "visual impression" based on how you look and your body language, specifically your facial expressions.

38% of the first impression is an "auditory impression" based on the sound of your voice and the way you speak your words.

7% of the first impression focuses on the feelings and attitudes of the words alone.

As you read the above research, it can give you the false idea that your words are the least important part of the conversation. Although that is not true, it is essential to note that **93%** of all face to face communication is non-verbal.

First Impressions, Rapport & Body Language

Since 55% of the first impression is perceived "visually" by how you look, let's begin by discussing body language as a "real" authentic language. Identical to other languages such as English, Italian, French, German, or Spanish, body language conveys genuine meaning. However, body language is a form of "nonverbal communication" in which physical behaviors, as opposed to words, are used to express, transfer, or convey information. These nonverbals may include facial expressions, shaking or nodding of the head, body posture, hand gestures, eye movement, eye contact, touching, a handshake, and space utilization.

"The most important piece of advice I can give you is to be sure that the words you're speaking (7%) are totally congruent with what your body language (55%) is transmitting."

If your mouth is saying one thing, but your body is saying something different, you send "mixed signals" to the person with whom you're communicating. These mixed signals create an instant breach in rapport and severely damage trust. I've conducted many interviews throughout my career and taught many seminars about doing well at your interview. And I'm amazed at how many very qualified candidates score poorly during their interviews because their body language is sloppy and incongruent with their spoken words.

For example, imagine telling a hiring manager how much you'd enjoy working for their company while your head is slowly turning from side to side, conveying a subliminal message of "NO." Imagine telling a hiring manager that you're flexible to work overtime while your head and facial expressions are indicating "NO." Imagine slowly shaking your head up and down, indicating "YES" from a body language perspective as your mouth answers "NO" when asked, *"Have negative customers ever caused you to lose your cool?"* Imagine someone telling you they love you and will always be faithful as their head shakes "NO." Imagine asking a car salesperson if the preowned car you're interested in has been in any accidents? Imagine they quickly respond "NO," but their head shakes up and down, indicating "YES." Be honest, wouldn't that make you feel uncomfortable? Wouldn't you feel a sense of betrayal? These are all examples of incongruent body language and poor communication skills.

Remember, anytime your body says something different than what is coming out of your mouth, you breach trust and rapport because of mixed signaling. What's even more interesting is that when preparing for an interview, many people invest most of their time deciding what they're "going to say." It's critical that you also rehearse your body language and be sure it's consistent with your verbal messaging. The moment you breach trust, especially in those first 15 seconds, your chance of a successful interview drops drastically.

It's hard to believe how much information a person can perceive or judge about you in only 15 seconds, but let's delve a little deeper. In just fifteen seconds, they will notice your hygiene, how well dressed you are, if you are wearing too much perfume or cologne, if you're excessive in your jewelry, if your clothes are clean and pressed, all the way down to if your shoes are polished. I realize this sounds harsh, but the hiring manager makes all these judgments to determine if you're the right person for the job. Does it now make sense why rapport is so important? Early in my career, I can remember trying to sell a package of seminars to a Fortune 500 company. Unfortunately, I went a little overboard with my cologne because the lady interviewing me had a severe allergic reaction to it. (I lost that deal.) Today, I look back on that painful memory, and I can laugh. But the day it happened, I was devastated and very humbled.

Communication research states that if you blunder the first impression, you have about four minutes to try and recover or win them over. Due to the power of selective perception, those four minutes will be tough for you. Selective perception shows that while you're trying to recover in those four minutes, the hiring manager is searching for more faults and looking for more things not to like about you. Principles in business etiquette teach that offering a professional apology in case of a blunder or slip-up can be ideal for recovering or bouncing back.

A Professional Apology Consists of 4 Steps

Step 1. You must quickly and sincerely say, *"I'm sorry."*
Step 2. You must genuinely ask for forgiveness.
Step 3. Assure that you will take every measure to prevent the problem from occurring again.
Step 4. (If necessary) Ask if you can somehow make it up to them.

In many cases, step 4 is not necessary. You only need to use this step if you've committed a major, colossal blunder. If not, the first three steps are appropriate. Be mindful that these steps are a model only; you may use your own words. However, the steps must always be used in the listed order. If you are dealing with a hiring manager educated in business etiquette and need to use this professional apology, I promise you it will impress them. While it's not a panacea, it's far more effective than sitting in the interview with egg on your face. I promise we will revisit these four steps in massive detail in chapter 8. Hopefully, you'll never need to use them.

Since 55% of the first impression revolves around your appearance and body language, the following are the top 5 visual things the hiring manager notices about you. Below is a quick "Rate Yourself Quiz." Use a pen and rate yourself on a scale of 1-3 on each of the first visual impressions. The low numbers will give you an indication of where you need to practice and polish yourself. Remember, the first impression takes only 15 seconds.

Top 5 Visual Impressions	**Rate Yourself:**		
	I'm **Poor!**	I'm **So-So!**	I'm **Great!**
1. Smile, Groomed Hair.	1	2	3
2. Well Pressed Clothes.	1	2	3
3. Polished, Un-scoffed Shoes.	1	2	3
4. Minimal Jewelry, Perfume or Cologne.	1	2	3
5. How you carry the entire package.	1	2	3

Soft Skills & Shaking Hands

The ability to properly shake hands is one of the many essential soft skills. Shaking hands is also an integral part of successful body language and rapport. Your handshake has an immediate impact on the first impression you create, and I've seen many people lose fantastic job opportunities due to a second-rate handshake. Much earlier in my career, I had a client tell me that I had the weakest handshake he'd ever experienced. He said something to me that I'll remember for the rest of my life. Are you ready for this one? He told me, *"I could never be truly successful unless I learn how to shake hands properly."* He also said that *"My handshake is more important than my resume."* Once again, I was devastated and humbled. It was not until that day that I realized how much your handshake reveals about you. People do not want to do business with someone who does not know how to shake hands properly; it's a turn-off, and it's gross. After that, I attended a mini-course on "handshaking etiquette" at the local college. Here are some interesting soft skill handshaking tips I learned in that mini-course.

Handshakes to Avoid

1. The Dishrag – This is when you shake with a weak, limp hand, and it feels like you're touching a wet, limp noodle. The dishrag gives the impression that you're creepy and is for wimps only.

2. The Bone Crusher – This is popular with men trying to demonstrate their masculinity. They usually squeeze extremely hard and don't let go until they hear a bone snap. If you have a weak, fragile, or arthritic hand, avoid shaking hands. Simply tell the other person your reason for avoiding their shake. They will surely understand, and it will not harm their first impression of you.

3. The Guided Missle – This is when they storm towards you at warp speed from fifty feet away with their hand and arm already extended. It's frightening!

4. The Jackhammer – This is when you vigorously shake the hand up and down in fast, rough motions like a power tool. If done correctly, you can dislocate the hiring manager's shoulder.

5. The Smother – Classified as placing your left hand on top of the person's other hand during the shake or using your left hand to hold their wrist or touch their shoulder. You need to be careful of this one because it can be misconstrued as sexual harassment. The fact is you never know who you are dealing with, so take caution and avoid this shake.

6. The Clammy Fish – Professionally known as the "grossest handshake" due to the hand's wet, moist, or sweaty surface. Sometimes there are legitimate reasons for a hand feeling wet. Usually, when someone's hand is wet, it could be they are nervous meeting you, or they are sick with the flu or fever. If you have a damp hand or are ill, avoid shaking hands. Simply tell the other person your reason for avoiding their shake. They will greatly appreciate it, and it will not harm their first impression of you.

How to Correctly Shake Hands in 4 Easy Steps

1. **Don't Shake the Fingers** - Never shake someone's fingers! It's called a "handshake," not a "finger shake." Make sure you take their entire hand in yours. You'll know you're grasping accurately if your thumb is touching theirs.

2. **Apply a Firm, Polite Grip** - There is no need to squeeze as if you are a compressor, and it's not necessary to break bones. If you hear a "snap," you're pressing too hard. Men in my classes often ask about applying less pressure when shaking a lady's hand? The answer is, "NO!" Apply a firm, polite grip to both sexes.

3. **Two or Three Shakes Total** - Shake only two or three times as you smile and give the person gentle eye contact.

4. Then, **Smoothly, Gently Let Go.** It's that simple!

Soft Skills & Eye Contact

Unfortunately, many people in the business world have taken the term "eye contact" literally. I've witnessed people stare into another's eyes as if they're Dracula trying to hypnotize them. Staring people down with direct eye contact is awkward, uncomfortable, and embarrassing. Worse, it makes you look like an unprofessional freak or weirdo. That type of eye contact is incorrect and can cause an instant breach in rapport.

The ability to give "Soft Eye Contact" is one of the many essential soft skills and an integral part of successful body language. Soft or gentle eye-contact means that you never stare into someone's eyes as if you are insane. Instead, your real objective is to gently look at their "entire face" without relentlessly focusing on their eyes. Remember if it's a gentle gaze-- it's eye contact; if you're staring-- it's stalking. Stop applying eye contact and begin practicing "face contact." Looking into someone's eyes and their entire face simultaneously is a better tactic. It is more gentle, kind, non-threatening, and friendly.

The Second Impression

The second impression immediately follows the first impression; however, as the first impression occurs in 15 seconds, **the second impression takes 45 seconds.** In the second impression, **they are judging 11 other things** about you, and at the end of **60 seconds total**, they have already decided to hire you or drop you.

The following is a list of the **Top 11 Impressions** hiring managers perceive about you.

1. Cleanliness – How clean are you? Here we have another visual impression, so they're noticing your hair, nails, clothes, shoes, breath, hygiene, and teeth.

2. Attractiveness – Also known as an "executive presence," and not necessarily how sexy you are. The real focus here is not on your "sexiness," but your "sex-appeal," or how professionally you carry the entire package.

3. Responsiveness – Do you have the ability to respond as quickly as possible to a situation? A hiring manager can determine your responsive skills based on how you answer questions during the interview.

4. Friendly – Are you happy? Do you smile? Do you have a sense of humor? Are you polite? Did you properly shake their hand? Are you using gentle eye contact? Friendliness is another essential soft skill and an indication you have a healthy personality.

5. Courteous - The adjective courteous comes from the Old French word "curteis," which means "having courtly bearing or manners." Courtly described the court nobles who hung around the castle and the entourage of kings and queens. So courteous behavior is a reminder of the value of good manners. Did you meet and greet with an optimistic statement? Did you say "please" and "thank you?" Did you mind your manners? Did you smile as you met the receptionist?

6. Knowledgeable – Here, the hiring manager decides if you're technically the right fit for the job and if you're teachable. Based on the job posting, do you have a firm grasp of the position's essential duties? Have you researched the company website so you can speak knowledgeably about the role and company? Have you shown your willingness to learn? Have you demonstrated your flexibility?

7. Sincere – The 7th observation during the forty-five-second 2nd impression is if you're sincere. Are your thoughts, words, body language, and actions reflective of a genuine person? Are you honest, heartfelt, open, and earnest?

8. Patient – Are you able to accept or tolerate delays, problems, or inconvenience without becoming annoyed or anxious? This is an indication of how you will treat team members and customers. You can accomplish almost anything if you have patience. You can even carry water in a sieve if you wait until it freezes. Patience is a valuable soft skill.

9. Confident - Confidence means feeling sure of yourself and your abilities — not in an arrogant way, but in a realistic, secure way. Confidence isn't about feeling as if you're superior to other people. It's a quiet inner knowledge that you're capable. Confident people are secure rather than insecure. The ideal way to project confidence is with your shoulders and an erect posture.

10. Empathetic – Do you demonstrate empathy? This is the ability to put yourself in someone else's shoes, the ability to understand and share the feelings of another. Empathy is another essential soft skill, especially if the company is searching for someone who must deal with demanding customers.

11. Professionalism - You never have to be concerned about projecting professionalism as long as you have mastered and demonstrated steps 1thru10. Professionalism is an encapsulation of all the rest.

Below is a quick "Rate Yourself Quiz." Use a pen and rate yourself on a scale of 1-5(1=least, 5=best) on each of the 2nd impressions. The low numbers will give you an indication of where you need to practice and polish yourself. Remember, on average, after the first 60 seconds, the hiring manager has almost made up their mind to hire you or pass on you.

The 2nd Top 11   Rate Yourself from 1-5 on Each Impression

1. Clean _____

2. Attractive _____

3. How responsive you are _____

4. Friendly _____

5. Courteous _____

6. Knowledgeable _____

7. Sincere _____

8. Patient _____

9. Confident _____

10. Empathetic _____

11. Professional   (Encapsulation of 1-10) _____

Chapter 3 Review

1. Rapport is the ability to create an instant personal connection with someone while simultaneously building a trusting relationship.

2. It takes only 15 seconds for someone to form a first impression of you.

3. It takes only 45 seconds for someone to form a second impression of you.

4. Combined, the first and second impressions require only 60 seconds.

5. If you blunder the first impression, you have only 4 minutes to recover.

6. Sadly, after the blunder, while you're trying to win them over, they look for more things not to like about you.

7. The ideal method for recovering from a blundered first impression is to offer a professional apology.

8. Usually, after the first and second impressions (60 seconds), they have already decided to hire you or pass on you.

9. Your body language must be congruent with your words, or you'll send mixed signals breaching trust and rapport.

10. Your handshake is considered body language and is as important, if not more important, than your resume.

11. We have converted the term "eye contact" to "face contact." We no longer stare into people's eyes; instead, we give their eyes and entire face a soft, gentle gaze.

Chapter 4

Soft Skills and a Positive Attitude

Harvard psychologist Williams James said: "The greatest discovery of our generation is that human beings can alter their lives by changing their attitudes."

You can't write a book about soft skills, people skills, or interpersonal skills unless you include a discussion about attitude. Your attitude plays a significant role in your professional and personal success and failures. Recently, the Carnegie Institute of Technology released a report stating that over 90% of employees fired shortly after being hired were let go because of a poor attitude. It seems that your attitude can get you hired-- and fired.

"A solid definition of attitude is how you communicate your mood to others."

However, as we will discuss in this chapter, your perceptions are more important than your attitude. Your perceptions create your attitude, and your attitude gives birth to your behavior.

Below is a five-step psychological model that neatly breaks down every life event's essential components or ingredients. It's called "The Anatomy of an Experience," similar to a model used in emotional intelligence training. You must learn to remain calm, cool, collected, and in "control" during difficult or challenging work events. Because your perceptions, attitude, behavior, and emotional intelligence play a significant role in getting hired and keeping your job.

The Anatomy of an Experience

1. EVENT – An expected or unexpected event occurs. The event can either be in or out of your control.

2. PERCEPTION – When an event occurs, we immediately perceive or pass judgment on that event. We create an internal representation of the event. We "attach meaning" to the event, determining whether it is good or bad, positive or negative. The event itself **DOES NOT** have any significance in your life. The event has no value in your life. No event has any consequence in your life until you attach a meaning to it. You need to place a perception or judgment upon events before they can have meaning. There are no right or wrong events, only how we perceive them.

In every event, there are at least two ways to perceive it, positively or negatively. The choice is always yours and in your control. For example, you can rejoice that thorn bushes have roses or complain that rose bushes have thorns. You can buckle your seat belt while thinking, *"I hope I don't get into an accident."* Or, you can buckle your seatbelt while thinking, *"This will keep me safe."* You can complain as you pay your bills or be grateful that you have the money to pay for them. You can focus on the donut or the hole. Sadly, most people focus on the hole and ignorantly blame the donut. Your perception is your point of power. Remember, we can't always predict or control the event, but we always have 100% control over how we perceive it.

3 ATTITUDE – Your attitude is a natural result of your perception. Our perceptions give birth to our attitude. The parent of every attitude is perception. Your attitude can vary from one situation to the next, but your perception controls those variables. When you work on correcting your attitude, you will only correct symptoms. When you work on changing your perceptions, you will correct the cause of the issue or problem. Changing your attitude will only bring temporary relief. Changing your perceptions brings permanent solutions. The happiest and most balanced people on Earth focus on maintaining their perceptions, not their attitude.

4. BEHAVIOR – Our behavior is a natural result of our attitude. Our attitude gives birth to our behavior. If your perception of an event is negative, that will lead to a negative attitude. If your attitude toward an event is negative, that will lead to negative behaviors. And how you behave always creates a brand new...

5. EVENT – Therefore, the entire process is cyclical; each step gives birth to the next in a never-ending circle. So what does all of this have to do with you? How can you benefit from learning and applying the above model? Is there good news? Yes, there is!

The good news is now that we understand our perceptions create our attitude, we can begin controlling and managing our attitude by quickly altering our perceptions. It's a matter of cause and effect. If you want to resolve a health issue treating the symptoms is not enough; you must also address the cause. You must treat the roots, not just the branches. The same is true if you're goal is to improve your attitude. You'll achieve faster and permanent results if you work on your perceptions first. Don't worry about changing how you feel (attitude) about things; instead, practice-changing how you see (perception) things. By merely changing your perceptions, your attitude automatically shifts with it. In other words, if you want to change your attitude and behavior, alter your perception first, and the other two will change without your help or efforts.

Here are a few examples to get you started:

Negative Perception

1. I have to go to work today.

Positive Perception

I'm grateful I have a job.

Negative Perception

2. They fired me today.

Positive Perception

They freed me up to do something better with my life.

Negative Perception

3. These customers complain all day.

Positive Perception

Without negative customers, I'd be unemployed.

Negative Perception

4. If they find out I was fired from my last job, they'll never hire me.

Positive Perception

Many people get fired from their jobs, and it is not a reflection of who I am.

Negative Perception

5. I have to pay $100,000 in taxes this year.

Positive Perception

Great news! That means I made a million dollars!

Using Questions to Alter Your Perceptions

As I mentioned earlier, no matter what event or situation pops up in your life, there are always at least two ways to view or perceive it. Positively or negatively. And the ultimate goal in developing a winning personality is to become a "perception shift genius." Meaning, when facing a challenging event, you must skillfully and quickly convert the negative perception to a more empowering one. The fastest method I know for rapidly altering perceptions is to practice asking yourself positive questions about the event itself. You'll notice if you ask yourself negative questions regarding the event, your perceptions will also be negative. If you ask yourself positive questions regarding the event, your perceptions will also be positive. Altering perceptions requires a little bit of practice, but it is effortless once you get the hang of it.

Below are some of the most powerful questions I've utilized to quickly alter my perceptions when surrounded by "perceived" difficult events or circumstances. Try them next time your attitude may get you into trouble.

A. *"What's funny about this?"*

B. *"What can I learn from this?"*

C. *"What can I do so this never happens again?"*

D. *"What is this lesson trying to show or teach me?"*

E. *"Are there any hidden benefits I'm overlooking in this event?"*

F. *"How can I quickly turn this situation around?"*

G. *"Is there a more positive way to look at this?"*

H. *"If a friend or loved one were in this situation, what advice would I give them?"*

Remember, the more positive your questions, and the quicker you can ask them of yourself, the more successful you'll be cultivating the winning attitude for landing and keeping a great job.

The 6 Qualities of a Healthy Personality!

Attitude and personality are cousins. Your attitude and personality are vital factors for creating a favorable 1st & 2nd impression at your interview.

Do you want to advance your professional and personal image? Do you want people to remember you by your confidence, flair, style, and, most of all, by your spirit? Your personality and how you project it is another soft skill for achieving these goals.

Your personality is the development of organized patterns, behaviors, and attitudes that make you distinct. Combined, they create a robust and attractive persona causing you to stand out and be remembered. In the corporate and public sectors, a pleasing personality can land a job and climb the success ladder much quicker than someone with a nasty or gloomy disposition. The candidate or employee with the personality of a dial tone rarely gets anywhere near the success ladder.

There are six distinct traits or qualities that people with healthy personalities possess. If you take a moment to reflect on some of our planet's most successful and memorable people, you will notice that they all had these six traits in one form or another. Even if your personality doesn't shine like a highly polished diamond yet, you'll be amazed at how much progress you can make in a very short time by knowing these traits. These behaviors are not reserved for only select people. The good news is everyone can develop a healthy personality with minimal time and practice. Let's take a look at the six qualities to understand better how easy it can be.

Quality # 1 - They Rarely Complain!

Logically, there is a time and a place for complaining. However, chronic complainers are chronic downers, and most people do not want to associate with them. It requires no musical talent to harp on something constantly. When necessary, healthy personalities complain in a "professional manner." That means: they wait for the opportune moment, they rarely raise their voices, are never derogatory, never point fingers, and most of all, they focus on solutions with "win-win" outcomes. If more people were trained to be "solution-oriented" rather than "problem-centered," complaining would become extinct.

Quality # 2 - They Easily Forgive!

It's very rare for a healthy personality to hold grudges. That's because they have a healthy self-esteem, which helps them not to take things personally. Although you cannot use them as doormats, a healthy personality is rarely plotting revenge or seeking to destroy anyone in any way. For the sake of your physiological and psychological health, always be mindful that it is far better to forgive and forget than to hate and remember.

Quality # 3 - They Get Along with <u>Lots</u> of <u>Different</u> Types of People!

Notice: They don't only get along with lots of people—they get along with lots of "different" types of people. That is an incredible soft skill that more people need to possess. Regardless of color, race, belief system, or sexual orientation, a healthy personality has excellent rapport skills and can find common ground with anyone. They usually build strong bonds with co-workers and friends, and this quality affords them healthy, long-term relationships.

Quality # 4 - They Maintain a Positive Mental Attitude! – (PMA)

The great Zig Ziglar said, *"Positive thinking will not help you do anything, but positive thinking can help you do **everything** better than negative thinking."* Therefore, a positive mental attitude at home and on the job is a critical component to your success. No one has ever suffered a severe eye strain case by looking on the bright side of things, which is what a healthy personality does so well. While they acknowledge or recognize negativity, they keep their eyes focused or fixed on the positive. Employees with a PMA climb the ladder of success faster than toxic, jaundiced, negative people.

Quality # 5 - They Are Assertive!

Assertiveness is another critical component of a healthy personality. Passive people violate their own rights and teach others how to harm them in the future. Aggressive people violate other people's rights to further themselves and their agenda. Assertive people promote everyone's rights simultaneously. Assertive behavior respects the needs and interests of all people. Instead of arrogance, they project a healthy sense of pride. Instead of greed, their focus is on achievement. Rather than competition, they think "win-win." A healthy personality is a natural result or byproduct of assertiveness. (We'll discuss assertiveness in greater detail in chapter 6.)

Quality # 6 - They Smile & Laugh A Lot!

The American Medical Association states that smiling & laughing creates many positive, healthy effects in your body. Laughing reduces your stress and helps to enhance immune functioning. A recent research report suggests that people with a highly developed sense of humor are less prone to illness. Did you know your smile can be a predictor of how long you'll live -- and that a simple smile has a measurable effect on your overall well-being? Smiling can help alleviate emotional pain and has a powerful impact on your mood. At the same time, your smile can change the attitude of others. The average preschooler laughs about 450 times per day, while the average adult laughs about 15 times per day. A person with a healthy personality smiles approximately 150-200 times per day. That could be the main reason why so many people gravitate towards them. Think back to your last interview. Were you smiling when you first met the interviewer? I hope so! Smiling is another indispensable soft skill. Remember, the direction of your day always goes in the direction that the corners of your mouth point. Therefore, laughter and smiling are the best medicine for "soul-ache" and must be taken in large doses. Perhaps we should all go back to preschool.

Attitude + Personality = Charisma

Are you charismatic? Charisma is the quality of being able to attract, charm, and influence those around you. It's an essential soft skill and something you need to project during your interview. It is usually easy to identify charismatic people. However, sometimes it can be challenging to pinpoint what skills or qualities those people have that other, less charismatic, people lack. Therefore, I'd like to offer you an acronym for the word "charisma." It's a simple way to remember some of the soft skills you can utilize to create your own "charismatic effect."

C – onfidence – we discussed confidence earlier, but as a reminder, the ideal way to project confidence is with an erect, shoulders back posture, a smile, and a good handshake.

H – appy – Happy means happy, NOT goofy.

A – wareness – During a job interview, you must demonstrate awareness and basic knowledge of the company, the position, and its goals. This kind of awareness is developed by reading the company's website before the interview.

R – espect - Respect is a way of treating or thinking about something or someone. You demonstrate respect by being polite and kind. Remember, you can respect "things" as well as people.

I – nspire – The ideal way to inspire your interviewer is in how you answer their questions. Great examples of how you saved your last employer money or took the initiative, or successfully lead a team are inspirational stories. We'll discuss this further in chapter 15.

S – ubtle – Another word for subtle is humble. Charismatic people possess all of these electrifying personality attributes, but they don't flaunt them or brag about them. If you are genuinely charismatic, you should not need to tell anyone you are. They should become aware of your abilities by merely being in your presence. Never tell people about your greatness; allow them to discover it for themselves. Remember, be humble or stumble.

M – otivate – Motivating a future employer is easy. Simply smile and project your eagerness to begin the new job. You can project passion, commitment, faithfulness, friendliness, and excitement. Motivated employees tend to get other team members motivated, so motivation is highly regarded and a necessary people skill.

A – ttitude – This has been the main focus of this chapter, but be mindful, negative attitudes attract negative people and events. Positive attitudes attract positive people and events. If you were a hiring manager, which one would you hire?

Land that Job by Developing Your Charisma Quotient:

Below is a quick "Rate Yourself Quiz." Use a pen and rate yourself on a scale of 1-5 (1=least, 5=best) on each charismatic characteristic. The low numbers will give you an indication of where you need to practice and polish yourself. Remember, your "Charismatic Aura" is projected by humbly integrating all of the below.

	Rate Yourself
Confidence	_____
Happy	_____
Awareness	_____
Respect	_____

Inspirational   _____

Subtle   (Humble)   _____

Motivational   _____

Attitude   _____

1- 2 – Your **Charisma Quotient is Very Low.** Choose two qualities where you gave yourself the highest score. Concentrate on developing these qualities first.

3- 4 – Your **Charisma Quotient is Average to High.** Chose two qualities on which you rated yourself a "3" and concentrate on improving these.

5 – Your **Charisma Quotient is Very Strong.** To use your charisma effectively, concentrate on the **"S"** element of the assessment.

The Law of Indirect Effort

I'm a big fan and proponent of the "Law of Indirect Effort." This law states that "you can always get what you want if you simply help enough people get what they want." Here are some ideas of how you can utilize the Law of Indirect Effort personally and professionally.

- If you want someone to be patient with you, first be patient with them.
- If you want someone to place value on serving you, first value them.
- If you want to be respected, you must first respect.
- If you want to be heard, you must first listen.
- If you want to be understood, you must first understand.
- If you want to be loved, you must first love.
- If you want someone to brag about you, first brag about them.
- If you want a compliment, you must first compliment.
- If you want someone to toot your horn, you must first toot theirs.
- If you want someone to be loyal, you must demonstrate your loyalty.
- If you want someone to boost your self-esteem, you must first boost theirs.

- If you want your team to be engaged, you must be engaged first.

Chapter 4 Review

1. Your attitude can get you hired and fired.

2. Your perceptions create your attitude.

3. Your perceptions are created by the positive or negative questions you ask yourself.

4. If you want to change your attitude, you must alter your perceptions.

5. If you want to change your perceptions, you must ask yourself positive questions during and after the event.

6. The goal is to become a perception shift genius.

7. Attitude + Personality = Charisma

8. Be humble or stumble

9. Hiring managers are hiring attitude and personality before technical skills.

10. The great thing about attitude is that you can change it!

Chapter 5

Soft Skills and Communication Mastery

"Communication is a verbal and non-verbal process of sharing information with another person in such a way that they understand what you are saying. Speaking, listening, and understanding are all involved in the process of communication." – Dr. Norman H. Wright

Communication has the potential of being a powerful positive tool in your repertoire of soft skills. Our verbal and non-verbal interactions often determine the success and failures of our interactions. Communication has two categories "Direct" and "Indirect."

Direct Communication is the "face to face" type of communication where both parties can see each other. They can hear each other's words and tone and can read each other's body language. The ability to read someone's body language is known as "Calibration." When you hear someone's words, you are "listening," and when you are reading body language, you are "calibrating."

Indirect Communication is known as "distant" communication when the communicators cannot see each other. Some examples could be communicating via text, email, snail mail, the telephone, or social media.

Humans have been verbally communicating for about 100,000 years and involved in written communication for over 25,000 years. The most popular language on Earth is Mandarin Chinese. The second is Spanish, and English comes in third. According to psychologists, the average one-year-old has a three-word vocabulary. By fifteen months, children can speak about nineteen words. At two years of age, youngsters have a working knowledge of about 272 words. A child's vocabulary catapults to about 896 words by the age of three. Then about 1540 words by the age of four, and 2072 words by the age of five. The average adult speaks at a rate of about 150 words per minute and up to 18,000 per day. However, this does not mean our words are clearly relayed or that rapport has been established.

Have you ever been involved in a conversation that seemed to flow effortlessly as you and your party seamlessly exchanged information? On the other hand, have you ever participated in the same type of exchange and felt like you were beating a dead horse? Have you ever been to a job interview and thought that you are not connecting with the hiring manager at all? The conversation seemed to be hitting a brick wall while you and the other party had no rapport?

These terrible communication traps happen all too often, especially in our business and personal lives. It seems that as we get caught up in our hectic, fast-paced day, the rules of effective communication get lost or forgotten. I follow an essential standard and teach the importance of regularly reviewing and practicing "the basics."

My research into the communication field demonstrates that eight cardinal bloopers frequently occur in communication processes. These eight bloopers can cause problem-solving to falter, relationships to crumble, hurt feelings, and breach rapport. They also project a negative attitude and personality. Communication encapsulates every other soft skill and is an art form. Let's review all eight bloopers, and as a rule of thumb, try to keep them "sacred" as we interact with others on a personal and professional level. My goal here is to enhance your communication abilities and, at the same time, boost your professional and personal interactions.

The 8 Primary Communication Bloopers!

Communication Blooper # 1 - Not Listening

Notice that this blooper is listed as number one because it's the most popular. It's natural for your mind to wander occasionally or for you to lose track of what someone is saying. For this mistake, you politely apologize and move on. However, deliberately not paying attention will cause a massive problem in your relationships. The primary goal of a communication process is to exchange information and, at the same time, build stronger relationships. These can be challenging ideals to achieve if you're not a good listener. If your goal is to start a new career, land a job, climb the corporate ladder, make the big sale, mediate conflict, or build better relationships---become a better listener.

Listening with Both Ears!

A horse walks into a bar, and the bartender asks, "Hey, why the long face?"

I heard the great comedian Frank Gorshin tell that joke in 1995. Hopefully, you remember him. His most famous acting role was as The Riddler in the Batman live-action television series of the 1960s. Perhaps the joke isn't that funny, but it does contain a lesson if you're listening with both ears.

Why would someone ask a horse such a stupid question? Isn't the bartender educated enough to realize that all horses have the same long face and head? Is it possible the bartender flunked out of his hippology classes? Was the bartender so drunk that he didn't realize that he was talking to a horse? Was the bar's lighting so dim that he didn't notice he was talking to a horse? I apologize for dissecting such a simple joke so unmercifully. However, all of that probing eventually led me to a satisfying answer, which will become our focus. The lesson here is the only people who would ask a horse about their long face are the people who are just not paying attention. Therein lies the first secret of being a good listener; **you have to pay attention to the person speaking to you.**

"The definition of listening is to give your full attention."

Unfortunately, instead of listening, most people are trying to think about what they're going to say next. This rude act turns your listening devices off, causing you to go into an internal daydream state. Many people drift so deep that they don't even realize the other person has stopped talking, usually followed by that awkward moment of dead, embarrassing silence. Many opportunities are missed because we are broadcasting when we should be listening. Remember, there are two kinds of bores---those who talk too much and those who listen too little. Hopefully, you're neither.

There are several soft skill strategies that you can employ to remain focused when you're required to listen and give your complete attention.

A. Body Language.

STOP whatever you're doing to avoid any distractions; it will be easier for you to hear and listen. **TURN** your full body towards the person speaking and try to

LEAN in slightly towards them as if what they're spouting is the most exciting information you've ever heard. While you never want to invade anyone's space, this is a useful tool to cue your mind to focus. **AVOID** distracting body language such as tapping your foot, clicking your pen, looking at your watch, staring out a window, and tapping your fingers. These behaviors can get you thrown out of an interview very quickly. They're also very rude.

B. Eye Contact. (Face Contact)

We discussed eye contact earlier, but it's worth repeating as a listening skill. Never look and stare directly into a person's eyes. Listening is not about stalking or creating an awkward staring contest. There's nothing worse than someone staring into your eyes as if they're trying to cast a spell on you. Looking directly at someone's face is more acceptable and less threatening than staring them down with constant eye contact; it's a softer approach. Eye and face contact are great tools because they allow you to observe the person's facial features as they are delivering their message. Watching someone's face and eyes will also enable you to view and hear what the person is **NOT** verbally saying. That is an essential strategy for listening with both ears. Always remember 93% of all communication is non-verbal and that people speak more with their body language than they do with their mouths.

C. Repeat their Words in Your Mind.

Here is another powerful but simple tool! As the person is speaking, occasionally repeat their words in your mind as if in playback mode. The repetition of the words sends a signal to your mind helping you to remain focused. It also improves your recall of the conversation and information. Instead of mentally, silently repeating their words, you might try visualizing a mental movie in your mind of what they're saying. I've used this strategy for many years, and I can attest that it enhances the art of listening and memory.

D. Don't Judge!

Another critical key for listening with both ears is not to judge the information as the speaker is transmitting it to you. Judgment turns your listening devices off, causing you to take an internal daydream trip to the land of criticism and assessment. As long as you're judging and pre-judging the incoming information, you may hear it, but you're not listening to it. Remember, listening takes both ears.

E. Give Verbal and Non-Verbal Responses.

This is significant! You must let the speaker or interviewer know that you're alive and that all the lights are on in your brain. There is nothing worse than speaking with someone who has the "deer in the headlight look" on their face. You must use your body language and smile, lean in closer, or nod your head as they are speaking. I call this giving someone a "visual." In other words, your body is signaling that you are focused and listening. You may also occasionally utilize non-verbals such as *"OK"* or *"Uh-Huh,"* but don't overdo it. Just remember, don't interrupt until they are finished. Take a tip from nature---your ears aren't made to close, but your mouth is! Remember, a closed mouth gathers no feet.

F. Paraphrase/ Restate

Paraphrasing is another popular soft skill and listening tool. It is utilized explicitly for obtaining clarity and helping you to understand the speaker's message thoroughly. Quite often, someone may say something to you, but your brain hears or interprets it differently than intended. Your job is to repeat back to the speaker what you think you heard or how you understood it for clarification. The speaker will then let you know if you heard correctly. Here are a few examples:

Hiring Manager – *"Our company is looking to hire a candidate who has impeccable people skills and a working knowledge of Microsoft."*

You – *"So if I hear you correctly, Microsoft and people skills are important proficiencies for your new hire?"*

Customer – *"I'm looking to purchase a car that gets good gas mileage and has a high safety record."*

You – *"If you're looking for a car that has an excellent safety record along with good gas mileage, I have just what you need."*

Your Supervisor – *"May I ask you to complete tasks A, B, & C and have them on my desk by Friday?"*

You – *"Sure! But to be clear, did you say tasks A, B, & D, or A, B & C?"*

As a special note, don't use paraphrasing after every sentence someone speaks. You'll drive each other crazy and waste precious time. The ideal time to paraphrase is if you feel you may have missed the message or a particular point. Perhaps your mind wandered, or there were distractions in the room, causing you to mishear. You also need to be cautious of your tone when you paraphrase. You never want your voice to sound sarcastic, frustrated, angry, or condescending. This may occur if you've already paraphrased the same point several times in a row. The purpose of paraphrasing is for clarity and connection. Frustrated and angry tones could cause the whole conversation to end up in the toilet.

Listed below, I have several listening questions. Take a brief moment and honestly answer each. If they help you notice a weakness, begin to focus on that area and correct it. In your business and personal life, listening or focusing your attention with both ears is a skill that cannot be neglected.

QUESTIONS:

1. Do you let people finish what they're trying to say before you speak?
2. Do you stop what you're doing and give 100% of your attention?
3. Do you give the person appropriate verbals & non-verbals as they speak?
4. Do you always listen with an open mind?
5. Do you begin rudely texting as a person is speaking?
6. Do you curb your own opinions, emotions, or judgments as they speak?
7. Do you talk about "nothing" just to fill in the silence?
8. Do you observe the person's body language (calibrate) as they speak?
9. Do you ask intelligent questions to clarify meaning?
10. Do you repeat their words in your mind?

I had a funny conversation with my dad recently. It was more entertaining than the joke about the horse. The best part is that it reinforces some of what we've just discussed. I've written the conversation out in script format to convey the humor better.

ME – *Hi, Dad! How are you?*

DAD – *Not good, not good, things are terrible and very bad!*

ME – *Why! What's wrong?*

DAD – *Well, you know how your mom tells those long, boring stories right in the middle of the baseball game, and I pretend that I'm listening?*

ME – *Yes.*

DAD – *Well, lately, after telling the long, boring story, she asks me to repeat everything she just said.*

Communication Blooper # 2 - Chronic Interrupting

This blooper is quickly resolved by just re-learning our manners. It's not polite to interrupt others while they are speaking. It demonstrates that you are a poor listener with a damaged self-esteem. It shows your lack of concern for the person speaking and sends a signal to others that you are rude. This mistake will cause you to lose credibility and job opportunities quickly! Credibility is essential when searching for a job.

Here are a few tips to help you control yourself from interrupting others.

A. Cross Your Fingers – I'm serious! Keeping your fingers crossed as someone is speaking can serve as a reminder to remain quiet until they have completed their thoughts. It's also very convenient because it's inconspicuous.

B. Bite Your Tongue – Try it; it works! Don't bite too hard where you might hurt yourself or bleed; just keep your tongue between your teeth and wait your turn.

C. Question Yourself – I have found this tool to be extremely valuable. While the other person is speaking, I ask myself, *"Can what I want to say wait?"* Or, *"Is what I'm about to say relevant and important?"* Most of the time, the answer is "no."

D. Count to 5 – When someone has stopped speaking, I have discovered it very dangerous to assume that they have finished. Sometimes they have not. They simply paused to take a breath or collect their thoughts. I always take this time to count from 1 to 5 silently. These extra few seconds create a safety factor so that when I interject my ideas, I'm not stepping on their toes. Please remember to count silently and don't move your lips.

Were you ever in a situation where you had to interrupt someone, perhaps in an emergency? Soft skills teach us that there are ways to interrupt someone that isn't rude or disruptive. The goal is to be polite. The most important thing to consider should you need to jump in and say something important is to show respect for other people. Here are a few soft skill tips for interrupting politely:

A. Have a Specific Purpose. Whether you are jumping into other people's conversation or you're disrupting someone's monologue, you must have a legitimate reason for doing so and the ability to relay the cause to the person talking. Remember, the moment you interrupt, immediately state the purpose as briefly as possible.

B. Get Your Timing Right – Unless you're interrupting because of an emergency, ask yourself, *"Is now the right time, or can it wait?"*

C. Interrupt with a Question – Polite questions usually precede polite interruptions. Some things you might say include, *" With your permission, may I interrupt for a moment?" "Excuse me," "I need to say something here," "Do you mind if I interrupt?" "I have an idea relating to what you just said," "I'd like to add something to that,"* or *"I beg your pardon, but I need to say something."* It's crucial to remember to thank the person or the group for allowing you to interrupt.

Communication Blooper # 3 - Criticism in Public

Today, in the training business, the term "criticism" has been keenly replaced with the words "coaching" or "feedback." Regardless, criticism in public is one of the fastest ways to annihilate your credibility, destroy your integrity, violate rapport, and lose friends. Please remember what I'm about to say now because it's crucial: *"You have no right, nor the authority to criticize any human being in public."* Anyone who has had any soft skills training understands that all criticism, feedback, and disciplinary actions must be conducted privately. The purpose of criticism or coaching is to build the individual's self-esteem while simultaneously correcting behavior. Therefore, during a coaching process, your focus must be on their behavior and the situation, never the person or their personality traits. We need to learn to separate the person from the problem. No matter how wrong a person may be, we must allow people to be "wrong with dignity" as a soft skill practitioner.

My first job after graduating from college was at the Federal Home Loan Bank in New York City. (I'll speak more about the bank in chapter 8.) I worked there for two years. Three months into my employment at the bank, I received my first performance review. Although my first three months were successful, I was also responsible for a few screw-ups, which I blamed on a learning curve. Therefore, as the day of my "first-ever" review approached, I was very nervous and anxious.

The actual review took about 30 minutes. My supervisor discussed my past performances, talked about goals for the future, and finally gave me a minimal list of what he called "things to be aware of." I believe this was a euphemism for "constructive criticism." He never said one negative thing about my blunders or my learning curve. In fact, at one point, it almost sounded as if he was complimenting my errors. He had a way of making my successes seem extensive and my mistakes small or insignificant.

I walked out of my first review feeling empowered, feeling good about myself, ready to move on to larger projects, and with a raise in pay. I'll remember that day forever. It has shaped how I deal with employees, clients, customers, and my family.

It's not always easy giving criticism to others, especially if it's a loved one. However, if you follow the three easy steps described next, I'm sure you'll find that the experience can be rewarding and sometimes a fun opportunity. As a footnote, if during a job interview, you are asked, *"What is your method for coaching or dealing with behavioral issues?"* Please answer by describing the following steps. I promise you will score big points at that interview and be looked upon very favorably.

3 Power Steps for Coaching a Behavior Correction

Step One – Save their Face.

Here is a very fundamental and essential step. Even though the person has warranted a coaching session, your job is to build their self-esteem and make them look good unless you're dealing with severe and dangerous behavioral issues. Your job is to approach the situation as if you are their coach, teacher, or mentor, not a judge and jury. It would be best if you approached with the mindset of helping---not belittling. Avoid negative, destructive phrases such as:

"No one in the history of this company has screwed up like this."

"Only an idiot can make a mistake like this."

"Your heart was in the right place, but your brain was out to lunch."

"This company must be flypaper for idiots."

"I see the screw-up fairy has revisited us."

Your job is **not** to rub their face in the mistake and make them feel worse than they already do. There is nothing worse than kicking someone when they're down. You can save their face and help them look good by opening the session with positive, constructive phrases such as:

"Don't feel bad; I made the same mistake once."

"This could have happened to anyone."

"Relax, we'll work on it together and create a solution."

"It's fine; let's just re-clarify your responsibilities."

I'm convinced that a significant part of the communication process is to help people feel better about themselves. Since you are the person about to deliver the criticism, you have a tremendous opportunity and obligation to help that person change their behavior or correct their problem through the process of construction—not destruction. This mindset will create trust, rapport, and credibility on your end, while the person on the receiving end basks in the comfort of your impeccable soft skills.

When you open a coaching session by saving someone's face, the rest of the process will flow relatively smoothly because the person will relax and drop their guard. When someone lowers their guard or their defenses, you'll find them in the perfect, receptive state of mind for step two.

Step Two-State Your Future Expectation.

Now that you've constructively explained the problem or situation at hand, it's time to explain what behaviors are expected in the future. That is called "stating future expectations." You might even consider brainstorming solutions together. This can be a creative method allowing the person to come up with some of their own solutions. Since the person is now relaxed and has dropped their defenses, you'll notice they are very receptive, eager to listen, and create solutions. The process has not hurt them so far, so they'll be ready to hear more of what you have to say.

Future Expectations for Behavior Modification Must Include 4 Steps:

A. The future intention must be specific.

B. The person must thoroughly understand what you are asking.

C. The person must have the ability to carry out the intention or goal—long term.

D. In business cases, the intention must be in writing. (Remember: if it's not in writing, it never happened.)

As an example, real future expectations might sound like this:

"Now that we've completely discussed the issue and you understand the problems it can create, here's what we expect from you in the future _____ (fill in the blank). Since this was a trap that anyone could have fallen into, I'm sure it won't happen again, and we look forward to more great work from you. Do you have any questions?"

Step Three – Thank Them & End It!

That's right! Thank them for listening and then end it—never bring it up again (unless the situation warrants it). You must demonstrate your trust in the person and their ability to carry through. Avoid monitoring their every move, looking over their shoulder, watching, or waiting for another mistake. That will make you crazy and them paranoid. They are now acutely aware of the problem; they have a plan to correct it, now it's time to let go and tend to new issues.

Graciously Receiving Criticism

I have never met anyone who enjoyed being criticized, even if it was disguised or softened with the word "constructive." Have you ever been unjustly criticized? Worse, have you ever been criticized by a blatant imbecile who has the people skills of a brain-damaged Neanderthal? I've met many of these.

The truth is that receiving criticism can provide valuable feedback, positively altering your life and career quality. It would be best if you changed the way you perceive it. Criticism can be an insightful gift that can put you on a higher road, save you time, and prevent you from making career-damaging mistakes. Although we may not always like what we hear, learning to respond to criticism with grace and dignity builds a solid character. In my soft skill seminars and my 2013 book, "Weapons of Mass Instruction," I share the **"4 Power Steps for Responding to Criticism."** The purpose of these actions is to help you use criticism to your advantage and prevent it from dragging you through the valley of embarrassment and self-pity.

4 Power Steps for Responding to Criticism

Step One - Become a Student.

You must remember that when you are being criticized, you need to *become a student*. Obviously, you are about to learn something about yourself or your behavior that you were not aware of earlier, and you need to adopt the attitude of a student eager to learn. You are about to discover something that can help you in the future. If you always keep in mind that the criticism you are about to receive can help you, you're less likely to get upset, angry, or defensive. Remember, becoming angry, defensive, or self-justifying only teaches your critic where your weaknesses are and how to hurt or upset you again in the future. Merely SHUT UP and POLITELY LISTEN WITHOUT INTERRUPTION!

Step Two - Politely Respond.

After your critic has had their say, then it is your turn to respond politely. You do this by paraphrasing back to the person what you think you've just heard and how you feel about it. That is the perfect time to explain the reasons for your behavior or lapse in judgment. If you have unintentionally hurt someone, it's also the ideal time for an apology. Keep focusing on your breathing and remaining calm. Clenching your fists or grinding your teeth is also not recommended. Keep your eye contact gentle.

Step Three - State Your Future Intentions.

Now that you've heard and politely acknowledged your critic, the most professional way to terminate the discussion is to state your positive future intentions. That can be a short, polite chat on how you'll utilize the newly disclosed information for everyone's benefit. Remember, revealing your future intention is an acknowledgment that you have fully understood the criticism and are planning to make the necessary changes to the very best of your ability. However, you must not fall into the trap of promising something that you cannot deliver. Be sure your future intention helps resolve the issue and is something with which you can take immediate action.

Step Four – Thank them

That's right! Always thank the coach or critic for bringing this valuable information to your attention. Simply saying, *"Thank you very much for bringing this to my attention,"* can work wonders giving you that professional soft skill edge.

Communication Blooper # 4 - Sarcasm & Ridicule

Sarcasm and ridicule rely heavily on body language, your tone of voice, and other non-verbal cues for effectiveness. Both are also very cynical and mean. Whereas criticism is aimed at personal behavior, sarcasm and ridicule are often negative remarks about the person. It is always rude and disrespectful to create some mockery or hurt someone's feelings. If your communication goal is to generate interconnectedness, rapport, and build self-esteem, avoid sarcasm & ridicule at all costs - especially in public. Kind words are the nicest thing we can offer to another person. Sarcasm trades kindness for cruelty. It serves no higher purpose, and it does not build self-esteem.

Communication Blooper #5 - Talking Down or Above Someone

Like sarcasm, ridicule, and criticism; this is another cardinal communication problem. It sends a message to the listener that you are smarter or more intelligent than they are. It conveys that you are above them in every way, while at the same time, it hurts feelings. The most important thing to remember is that talking down also conveys that your self-esteem is severely damaged. There are two ways to have the tallest building in the city: First - build the tallest building, or second - knock everyone else's building down. How do you want to be remembered --- as a builder or a destroyer?

Communication Blooper # 6 - Pompous Word Usage

These are large words used in a conversation that you know the listener will not understand. These include all types of jargon, slang, lingo, and "$50 words used in a 5 cent conversation." Pompous word usage is one of the fastest ways to turn a listener off since it creates an awkward separation between you and your listener. There are two types of people who use pompous words: First is the person who is so highly educated, they know of no other way to express themselves. (We can forgive these folks.) The second is the person who is only trying to impress you. Factually, using pompous words can make you appear arrogant. Remember, it is extremely obfuscating to promulgate any complex or lengthy lexicon. (HA!)

Communication Blooper # 7 - Gossip of Any Kind

My parents taught me to never talk about anyone behind their back. Never say anything about anyone that you would not say to their face. No matter how you look at it, gossip is improper. Spreading malicious rumors will not only hurt the subject of the gossip, but it also makes you look rude and immature. It also makes the person or people listening to your gossip uncomfortable. Or at least it should.

When you gossip about others, you do not define them; you define yourself as someone who needs to gossip. And everyone who has witnessed your gossip now knows you are "that" type of person. Avoiding gossip defines your character and advances your professional image.

Most people gossip to get attention and feel better about themselves, but it typically backfires on the gossiper and those willing to stand there and listen. No one ever benefits from a malicious discussion about other people. It's also time that could be better spent doing or saying something positive. I've seen many gossips lose their jobs; it's the antithesis of soft skills. We'll revisit this in chapter 7.

Soft Skill Tips to Prevent Gossip

A. Walk away – Your professional reputation is invaluable, and you cannot allow it to be tarnished by involving yourself in gossip. The fastest way to signal to a gossiper that you are not interested in the malicious discussion is to turn and walk away. The essential time to walk away is when the gossip turns to trash talking. They'll get the message quickly. However, as a word of warning, you may be the star topic in their next gossip gathering.

B. Stick up for the person – If the gossip is a lie, speak up and say so politely. If the gossip is valid, defend the person in the same manner you'd like someone to defend you. You can also politely say, *"If we can't speak this way to their face, we should not be speaking this way when they are not here."* Your character's true test is how you speak about someone when they are not there to hear. These are the kind of people who get hired on the spot.

C. Avoid whispering- Whispering can always be misconstrued; even if you're not speaking behind their back, whispering can still hurt someone's feelings.

D. Quickly change the subject – The moment someone begins gossiping, intentionally change the subject. If the gossiping begins again, say, *"I don't think it's professional to speak about someone if they are not here to defend themself."* If they're smart, they'll get it and shut up.

Communication Blooper # 8 - Making Yourself More Important

This final communication blooper neatly sums up or encapsulates the last seven. You are well on your way to rock-solid communication skills and healthy relationships if you approach everyone as if they are your equal. The fact is - they are!

I mentioned earlier that the most critical communication rule I follow is regularly practicing and applying "the basics." Memorize these eight bloopers and then do the **opposite** of each. Keep these communication soft skills "sacred" as you interact with others personally and professionally.

Chapter 5 Review

1. Be a good listener.

2. Speak when it's your turn.

3. Avoid criticism in public.

4. Avoid sarcasm and ridicule.

5. Speak to people at their level.

6. Use easy to understand terminology.

7. Speak kindly of others.

8. See everyone as your equal.

9. When someone speaks to you, immediately STOP what you are doing and turn your full body towards them.

10. Practice good face & eye contact. Never stalk anyone with your eyes.

11. Repeat their words silently in your mind.

12. Don't judge!

13. Give verbal and nonverbal acknowledgments.

Soft Skills Communication Quiz

Answer "Yes" or "No" For Each Statement

1. I feel comfortable starting a conversation with strangers.   Yes/No
2. I know how to put people at ease.   Yes/No
3. I'm good at remembering people's names.   Yes/No
4. I know how to smooth out a sticky situation.   Yes/No
5. I know when I've gotten through to the other person.   Yes/No
6. I know how to use my voice to make my message clear.   Yes/No
7. I'm prepared for any reaction when I give feedback.   Yes/No
8. I can disagree with someone and not get into an argument.   Yes/No
9. I stay calm when other people get upset.   Yes/No
10. I know when to shut up and let others speak.   Yes/No
11. I'm good at reading body language. (Calibration)   Yes/No
12. I can sense when someone has had enough of me.   Yes/No

Evaluating your score:

- If you responded **"yes" to 10-12** of the questions above, you are an excellent communicator.

- If you responded **"yes" to 7-9** of the questions, you are good but still have room to grow.

- If you responded **"yes" to 6 or below,** you need to polish your skills.

Chapter 6

Soft Skills and Assertiveness

In chapter 4, we briefly touched upon the topic of assertiveness. I promised we'd discuss it in more detail because it is another essential soft skill. While I dislike labeling people, I do find this topic to be quite significant. At a closer look, perhaps this chapter is not labeling people; instead, it's isolating people's behavioral style and how it affects their lives and success.

The three behavior styles I'd like to address and focus on are:

The Passive

The Aggressive

The Assertive

While each style is unique and has distinct characteristics, every human being has each style alive within themselves. The style most dominant in your personality usually fluctuates according to the situation or occasion. That is quite normal.

However, a severe personality issue arises if a person favors one style without shifting or pivoting to the others when required. Suppose you are locked into one dominant style without the flexibility to utilize the others at a moment's notice. In that case, it can dramatically affect your dealings with people on a broad scale. Let's take a look at all three styles:

The Passive – This is sometimes the dominant pattern of someone with damaged self-esteem. The Passives have a nickname, **"D.O.O.R.M.A.T.S,"** which is an acronym for "The Dependent Order Of Really Meek And Timid Souls." While on a behavioral level, "meek and timid" are quite socially acceptable, it sadly lends itself to be taken advantage of if you can't shift to your aggressive or assertive styles when needed. Passive is sometimes useful, as long as you are not locked and trapped in that style.

Psychologically, passive people violate their rights and, in doing so, teach other people how to hurt them in the future. That, unfortunately, creates a "victim mentality." Passive folks choose to be victims.

Passive **thinking** reflects, *"I'm not good enough."*

Passive **words** reflect, *"I can't."*

Passive **mind** reflects, *"You're OK; I'm not."*

Passive **actions** reflect – Silence.

The Aggressive – This is also the dominant pattern of someone with damaged self-esteem. Psychologically, aggressive people violate everyone's rights without regard to circumstance or outcome. They usually display a healthy arrogance, notable as an inflated sense of self-importance about condition or status. However, this arrogance is simply a cover-up for many insecurities. Also known as bullies, this personality style can be instrumental in particular threatening or hostile situations. However, it is the least socially accepted of all three. While passive people violate their rights, aggressive people violate other's rights. While passive people choose to be victims, aggressive people create victims.

Aggressive **thinking** reflects, *"I'm better than you."*

Aggressive **words** reflect, *"You make me angry."*

Aggressive **mind** reflects, *"I'm hot; you're not."*

Aggressive **actions** reflect – Shouting.

The Assertive – This is the dominant pattern of someone with healthy self-esteem. Assertiveness is the most socially accepted of all three styles because they promote everyone's rights simultaneously. Assertive behavior respects the needs and rights of all individuals or parties. Instead of arrogance, they display pride, also known as a healthy sense of your dignity. The assertive person represents how they think and feel with no apology for expressing their emotions or thoughts. They refuse to be manipulated by false guilt and never sacrifice others' rights to get what they want or need.

This type of "unity thinking" allows them to be accepted and successful in all areas due to a high level of trust. People want to associate with them, do business with them, and hire them because they work well with teams, and they've got your back.

Assertive **thinking** reflects, *"We're all important."*

Assertive **words** reflect, *"I believe we can."*

Assertive **mind** reflects, *"We're both OK."*

Assertive **actions** reflect – Calm.

To develop a more assertive personality, you must first establish three "sub" behaviors. Sub-behaviors are the foundation and substance of assertiveness.

The Three Cs of Assertiveness

1. Courage – The courage to stand up for yourself and others while effectively managing your boundaries. Courage is feeling fear yet choosing to act.

2. Connection – The ability to positively influence people and move them to "win-win" outcomes through motivation, not manipulation or fear. The capacity to let people know you are on their side through thick and thin.

3. Caring – This is done with eye contact, smiling, sharing, being true to your word, and helping those who can't help themselves.

Assertiveness and Job Searching

Assertiveness is a desirable quality to possess when hunting for a job. It increases your market value, and it's in very high demand if you're searching for a leadership position. Here are several tips to help you be a more assertive job seeker, even if your personality is the exact opposite:

1. Recognize Your Value.

Besides your resume, you need a separate, personal list of all your skills, achievements, positive qualities, and beneficial competencies. This list can help make your job search more comfortable because it will enhance your confidence levels and increase your momentum. The list must contain everything you bring to the table, and everything you believe makes you qualified for the jobs you're seeking. Write out everything you can think of from computer skills, customer service skills, language skills, and more. Be sure you incorporate all of this information onto your resume and your professional social media platforms.

That essential list will bolster your self-assurance reminding you that you are deserving of a high position. This will help you be more assertive and self-assured when your next interview rolls around. To maintain high enthusiasm levels, hang the list where you can see it and read it daily.

2. Avoid Weak Terminology.

Confidence, self-assuredness, articulate, and well-spoken are several characteristics displayed by assertive people. For that reason, you'll want to eliminate weak terminology from your vocabulary.

What do I mean by "weak terminology?" Words like "sort of," "kind of," "might," "pretty good," "not so bad," and many others fit the bill. Weak terminology diminishes your persona and your message, especially at an interview. Weak language can give the impression that you are too passive or uncertain about your abilities. Here are a few examples:

Weak - *"I sort of led a team once, and it turned out OK."*

Strong - *"Yes, I have successfully led a team. I earned all of the respect from my team members, and we were very successful at reaching our objectives."*

Weak - *"I'm pretty good at typing up proposals."*

Strong - *"I enjoy working on proposals, and I'm very effective at putting them together."*

Weak - *"Customers kind of like me."*

Strong - *"I enjoy working with customers, and I'm sure they enjoy working with me."*

Did you notice how the stronger statements assertively consider the needs of both parties? That type of direct language pattern can make a massive difference in the way you present yourself at an interview. Starting today, begin making a conscious effort to be more direct, sharp, and concise in your choice of words, and you'll project far greater assertiveness.

The Assertive Peasant

"In ancient times, a king had his men place a boulder on a roadway. He then hid in the bushes and watched to see if anyone would move the boulder out of the way. Some of the king's wealthiest merchants and courtiers passed by and simply walked around it.

Many people blamed the King for not keeping the roads clear, but none did anything about getting the stone removed.

One day, a peasant came along, carrying vegetables. Upon approaching the boulder, the peasant laid down his burden and tried to push the stone out of the way. After much pushing and straining, he finally managed.

After the peasant went back to pick up his vegetables, he noticed a purse lying in the road where the boulder had been. The purse contained many gold coins and a note from the King explaining that the gold was for the person who removed the boulder from the road."

You will encounter many boulders on your job search. Proactively and assertively, keep pushing them out of your way, and you'll soon be rewarded with a much-deserved paycheck.

Chapter 6 Review

1. Passive people violate their rights and victimize themselves.

2. Aggressive people violate your rights and victimize you.

3. Assertive people promote everyone's rights simultaneously. There are no victims.

4. Passive-aggressive people victimize themselves and others.

5. Assertiveness has a direct link to your confidence levels.

6. It's easy to work with assertive people because they watch your back.

7. It's easy to admire assertive people because they watch your back.

8. It's easy to problem-solve with assertive people because they watch your back.

9. Assertiveness focuses on "we" rather than "me."

10. Assertive people use bold, direct language patterns.

11. In a few cases, a passive style can be useful, as long as you are not permanently locked into it.

12. In a few cases, an aggressive style can be helpful, as long as you are not permanently locked into it.

A Possible Interview Question:

"What would you say is your greatest strength?"

Your Possible Answer:

"I believe my greatest strength is my assertive communication style. My assertiveness has helped me deal more effectively with difficult customers. It has also helped me get along with different types of people and mesh well with various team styles. I also believe that when you look out for others as well as yourself, it builds trust, rapport, and credibility, essential qualities for any leader."

(Be prepared to give a recent example.)

Chapter 7

Applying Soft Skills to Negative People!

The Parable of the Frogs and Pit

A group of frogs were traveling through the forest when two of them fell into a deep pit. When the other frogs saw how deep the pit was, they told the two frogs that there was no hope left for them.

However, the two frogs ignored their comrades and began trying to jump out of the pit. Despite their efforts, the group of frogs at the top were still saying that they should give up as they'd never make it out.

Eventually, one of the frogs took heed of what the others said, gave up, and died. Upon seeing this, the other frog continued to jump as hard as he could. Once again, the frogs yelled down at him to stop the pain, stay there, accept his fate and die.

He ignored them, and jumped even harder, and finally made it out. After escaping, he thanked the frogs for the fantastic encouragement. The other frogs asked, *"Did you not hear us?" "We were screaming for you to let go and die because there was no hope."*

The frog explained that he was deaf and that he thought they were encouraging him the entire time.

The moral of the story is sometimes you need to turn a deaf ear and ignore the negative.

What is Negativity?

In an earlier chapter, I mentioned that Corporate America spends over 3 billion dollars a year dealing with negative workplace employees. More people are fired from their jobs because of the repercussions of negativity, a poor personality, gossip, backstabbing, tantrums, bullying, mood swings, and aggressiveness than for any other reason. That's why people skills or soft skills are in such high demand. Soft skills are a valuable tool for softening up difficult people. And if you possess the knack for dealing with negativity, you will be a precious, hirable employee.

Have you ever worked with at least one negative, toxic, low-life, jaundiced, downbeat, depressing, venomous, jaded, cynical person? As you drive into your office parking lot and see their car, do you get pissed?

Negative people, also known as "Toxic Vampires" (TVs), find it very difficult to maintain their jobs in today's climate. Sadly, there's at least one in every family, every business, and every team. You can place one Toxic Vampire on a team of twenty-five people, and their negativity can quickly destroy team morale and productivity. They always see the dark side of things, are chronically aggressive, regularly use negative terminology, and have the personality of a wet mop.

Are there any strategies for effectively working with these characters? Are there any coping techniques to apply if you live with or are married to a TV? There's an old expression about "walking a mile in someone's shoes," and I believe this can help us understand why TVs act the way they do. Truthfully, once we understand someone's internal programming, it's easier for us to have some mercy on them.

For our purposes, we will define negativity as *"out of control pessimism."* There are two types of negativity: "Situational" and "Chronic."

Situational Negativity is a realistic, healthy, natural response to any unexpected or fearful circumstance. Situational negativity is relatively healthy because it allows you to vent or mourn in a controlled manner. It also protects you by keeping you vigilant and on your toes. Once the negative event passes, most people release the negativity and move on with their lives.

Chronic Negativity is similar to situational, except, in this case, TVs hold on to the negativity, dwell on it, and **NEVER** let it go. They live it, breathe it, and talk about it. They also enjoy company, so they are continually looking for recruits. By spreading negativity to others, it helps them feel less lonely and gives them a false sense of power and control.

Negative thinking is a behavior learned at an early age by modeling our parents, television stars, friends, and teachers. All underachievers maintain a negative attitude. Their negativity allows them to lead a mediocre life without guilt. Negative thinking serves as an internal coping mechanism that protects them from disappointment and fear. Their negative ideology acts as a "protective mechanism." When failure, discontentment, or misfortune happens in a TVs life, their negative attitude can ease the blow-and even justify it. In other words, all negative behaviors are utilized for some subconscious "pay off."

"These negative behaviors are mal-adaptive defenses of the ego."

These defenses were learned and worked successfully in their younger, formative years, but are no longer appropriate as an adult.

The Know It All

As an example, I'm sure you work with at least one **"Expert-Know it all."** They know everything about everything (at least they think they do). Working with this personality can be difficult. However, as with all negative behavior, it's used as a protective mechanism and a cry for help. The "know it all" is utilizing that false front to cover up insecurity. By acting smarter than they are, they hope that you won't realize that--- they are not. Their "payoff" is the belief that they won't be "found out." Remember, a "real expert" has something to say, while the "know it all" just wants to say something. In reality, the genuine expert never has to tell you that they are.

Once you psychologically understand why the "know-it-all" behaves the way they do, it can be sad. Some may even feel sorry for them. While that doesn't excuse their behavior, it should remind you that they need to be treated objectively as someone with whom you should take caution.

The Control Freak

Another favorite TV is the **"Control-Freak."** You may know one of these, and as with all TVs, this is another personality born out of fear. They deliberately control situations that *they already know they can handle* to reinforce their false sense of power to themselves and others. In this case, their payoff is the safety in not being found out that they feel powerless. Once you psychologically understand why the "control freak" behaves the way they do, it can be sad. Some may even feel sorry for them. While that doesn't excuse their behavior, it should remind you that they need to be treated objectively as someone you must deal with cautiously.

Chronic Complainers

What about **"Chronic Complainers?"** This TV cries, whines, and moans all day long about everything. Their favorite pastime is giving co-workers headaches. You may have heard the expression, "the squeaky wheel gets the grease." The expression of the chronic complainer is, "the squeaky wheel gets the---gifts!" The gifts they so desperately desire are *"attention"* and *"to be heard."* Chronic complainers believe that no one likes them, and complaining is their tool for getting noticed. In other words, they'd rather have negative attention than no attention at all. Once you psychologically understand why the "chronic complainer" behaves the way they do, it can be sad. Some may even feel sorry for them. While that doesn't excuse their behavior, it should remind you that they need to be treated objectively as someone you must deal with cautiously.

The Gossip

"The Gossip" in your office is suffering from a sad case of loneliness. That is why they generously spread the latest news and rumors around the office. Therefore, gossip is a tool used to get attention and to feel superior. The idea is that I know something you don't, and I have the power to decide whether or not to share it with you. They also use gossip as a "here's my gift to you" approach if they're trying to get you to like them. Once you psychologically understand why the "gossip" behaves the way they do, it can be sad. Some may even feel sorry for them. Again, while that doesn't excuse their behavior, it should remind you that they need to be treated objectively as someone you must deal with cautiously.

The Back-Stabber

The most dangerous of all TVs are **"The Back-Stabbers,"** because, unlike the others, they deliberately hurt people. Unlike the others, the back-stabber is also a real coward because they intentionally hurt you when you're not looking or not around. These people are so unhappy with themselves and their life situation that they have no emotional resources. They use back-stabbing as a tool to get control and to feel falsely empowered. As sad as that sounds, therein lies your revenge. You must take that power away from them. Therefore, the most efficient way to deal with a back-stabber is an immediate confrontation. The longer you wait to confront them, the more damage they can do. A quick confrontation shows them that you have no fear and they can't hurt you. The moment a back-stabber realizes they can't harm you, they'll retreat and leave you alone, realizing they won't get any empowerment from you.

There are plenty of informational resources available to teach you every strategy you need to know about dealing with negative people. However, I would like to give the entire issue a soft skill twist. I have three steps that I've successfully applied to difficult, negative people that I'd like to share with you now. At least one of the three steps has helped me in **EVERY** negative encounter. These actions may differ from what you've used in the past. However, work with it and let me know about your successes.

1. Ignore it!

Sometimes you need to be like the deaf frog. As over-simplistic as this sounds, if you are in a position where ignoring the TV benefits you, then take that route. You don't have to fight every battle that comes your way. Again, you don't have to fight every battle that comes your way. However, there are seven specific instances when you should not ignore negative behavior.

A. The TV is diminishing your ideas.

B. The TV is harming your reputation.

C. It's for the betterment of the organization.

D. You're standing up against action that is cruel or illegal.

E. Something legitimate or essential is at stake.

F. The issue involves your integrity.

G. The issue involves a significant amount of money.

If you can't ignore it, then apply the next two steps.

2. Protect Yourself from them.

If you can't ignore them, then you must protect yourself. That is done by not allowing TVs to learn that they have affected you in any way. Even if you have to fake it, never let them know that they got to you. They look for people's buttons and weaknesses. They are always searching for a path into your head, and if you expose your buttons, they will be happy to push them. TVs are looking for easy victims. Once they realize they can't suck you into the gutter with them, they quickly move onto another victim. If you don't want anyone to get your goat, don't let them know where it's tied up. If they already know where your goat is---then MOVE IT! Do not expose your buttons to a TV.

3. Try to Help them.

This one is my favorite, and I've been successful with it many times. I confidently and politely confront the person about the issue or situation and ask them if there's any way I can help. It's an assertive approach. If they tell me to go to hell, I go back and apply step one. If they seem gracious and welcome the assistance, I'll go out of my way to try and make their life better.

Even though TVs reveal themselves in different personality styles, there is one other interesting fact that they all have in common.

"Negative people do not know that they're negative. Negative people think they're positive."

That fact now leads us to you. Is it possible you're a TV and don't realize it? That is very common, and you may need to do a reality check on yourself. Sometimes we're so busy minding other people's negativity that we let ours go unchecked and out of hand. That can cost you your job. Is it possible people are talking behind your back? Can it be when people see you coming, they duck into another room? Suppose you're the one in the office who is perceived as being negative?

There are three steps you can apply that will help you bounce back and recover.

1. Ask Your Most Trusted Friends for Feedback.

Just ask, *"Do you think I'm negative in any way?"* If they respond that you do have TV tendencies, you mustn't *destroy the messenger*. Remember, do not let anyone know where your buttons are. Please don't get upset or angry with them, and most of all, don't defend yourself. You asked them for help, and they graciously gave you the answer. The best response is to be a student, listen carefully, take it all in, learn, and then politely thank them.

2. Continuously Monitor Yourself.

Develop a checklist based on information gathered from your friends and track yourself. Continue to ask your friends for feedback or progress status, and reward yourself as you slowly make the required positive changes.

3. Always Look for Opportunities to be Positive and Optimistic.

Find positive things to say and do, even if at first you have to overdo it a little. Read positive and uplifting books to shift your moods. Most of all, stop hanging out with TVs. You never rise higher than the people you associate with, so you may need to change your friends. Over 32% of pay raises and promotions are suspended because managers correlate people with their negative friends. Birds of a feather go broke together.

Self Reflection – Are You Guilty of Any of These?

The following 15 points are placed here as a "point of self-reflection." Carefully read them and deeply examine yourself. Even if you get hired, these toxic habits and behaviors can quickly steer you in the direction of instant termination.

You are a Problem Employee and Toxic Vampire if You:

1. Spread rumors, gossip, lie, speak condescendingly, or backstab.

2. Plagiarize other people's work or steal their ideas.

3. Have regular temper tantrums.

4. Burn your bridges.

5. Constantly bring smelly food into work.

6. You often brag.

7. You perceive your manager as your enemy.

8. You can't find a manager willing to give you a reference.

9. People do not want to work with you.

10. You've disliked every job you've ever had.

11. You're convinced you're the smartest person in the company.

12. You're "problem-centered" rather than "solution-oriented."

13. You complain without offering solutions.

14. You whine.

15. You say, *"It's not my job,"* at least once a week.

Soft Skills Strategies Review for Dealing with Negativity

DO NOT ignore negative behaviors.

INSTEAD, quickly confront and encourage dialogue.

DO NOT dictate or argue.

INSTEAD, suggest, consult and coach.

DO NOT "hint' or "snipe" about negative behaviors.

INSTEAD, confront the behavior directly.

DO NOT focus on the "extremes of negativity."

INSTEAD, create clarity, clarify and focus on specifics.

DO NOT get personal.

INSTEAD, stick to the issues and focus on your goals.

DO NOT take things personally.

INSTEAD, take things professionally while maintaining your perspective and some humor.

In the corporate world, optimistic people climb the ladder of success much faster than TVs. Optimists remain in their jobs for extended periods and have a lower turnover rate. My observations have been, the more you monitor yourself and the more positive you are, you'll remain employed for years to come.

Dealing with negative and challenging people is an intense subject. Therefore, I will cover the confrontation and problem-solving topics more thoroughly in chapter 10, Dealing with Conflict.

Chapter 7 Review

1. Negativity is out of control pessimism.

2. Situational negativity is healthy and natural.

3. Chronic negativity is an unrealistic response to external events.

4. Negativity is a learned behavior.

5. All negative behavior is rewarded with a subconscious payoff.

6. Negative reactions are mal-adaptive defenses of the ego.

7. You don't have to fight every battle that comes your way.

8. Your promotability factor increases if you are positive and optimistic.

9. Keep your buttons hidden, and do not let TVs push them.

10. You never rise higher than the people with whom you associate.

11. Birds of a feather lose jobs together.

Chapter 8

Soft Skills and Customer Service

Are you ready for a mini-course about customer service? Why? Because customer service and soft skills are identical twins. It doesn't matter which career you choose or the position you are applying for; you will always be involved in some type of customer service daily. However, there is another method to my madness. Since soft skills are such an essential part of the hiring process, I've designed this chapter to offer possible answers to probable questions you'll be asked at your interview. For your benefit, I'm going to present you with a wide variety of customer service concepts to prepare you for your interview. I firmly believe that if you answer your interview questions with a "service-centered mentality," it will dramatically increase your market value. In many cases, it can help you earn a higher than expected income during your salary negotiations.

In chapter 15, we are going to discuss how to answer specific interview questions confidently and accurately. However, I've received thousands of emails from students who have attended my training. They all report that they borrowed insights from this chapter to answer difficult interview questions and eventually landed the job successfully. Remember, soft skills are your key. So, keep a highlighter handy, and let's begin learning some customer service strategies that will help you be more successful at your interview, performing your job, or starting your own business. At the end of this chapter, I will ask you some probable interview questions based on this material.

What is Customer Service?

The term "customer service" is old and outdated. Today, in such an overly competitive market, providing good customer service will barely help you get your foot in the door. If you want to succeed in business, you must put all of your focus on the "customer experience." It's all about building relationships. If you ask a thousand people to define customer service, you'll get one thousand different answers. My definition is:

"To provide an expectation shattering experience combined with an attitude of gratitude for the sole purpose of converting customers into apostles."

Good customer service is not enough to create a thriving, prosperous business. Today's marketplace is super competitive, and a company cannot survive on good customer service alone. To achieve the "pinnacle of success" and remain ahead of the pack, Corporate America needs to shift its thinking away from customer service and magnify its focus on creating euphoric and loyal relationships with its customers. Excellent customer service should be a byproduct of the loyal, strong relationships you have built with the people supporting your business -- not the other way around. Personally, I enjoy receiving good customer service, yet the companies that I consistently prosper are the ones who treat me like I'm family. I feel very strongly about this, and it's the focal point of my business philosophy.

Whenever my car needs gas, I travel an extra five minutes down the road because the employees at that station treat me as if I'm family. There are other filling stations closer to my home, but they're not friendly. The employees lack fundamental soft skills. They never smile or say hello. They rarely look at me or say thank you when taking my money. So, I happily brought my business elsewhere. There's an old expression, *"Treat your customers like gold."* Of course, I disagree with that. My philosophy is to treat your customers "better than gold." Treat them like family. Why? Simply put, our customers do more for us financially than our families do.

I have a beautiful family; they are the most fabulous family in the world. However, my family doesn't pay my mortgage or my electric bills. My family doesn't put gas in my car. My family doesn't buy my clothes or pay for my daughter's school bills. Can you guess who pays all my bills? That's correct! My customers pay all my bills and allow me to lead the kind of life I do. The wonderful people who purchase my books and attend my seminars pay my bills. And to thank you for your loyalty, I will continuously strive to treat you with respect, giving you the best customer experience possible. I call this an "attitude of gratitude."

Mr. Anthony Gigante is a dear friend of mine and a very successful entrepreneur. He recently told me that his rise to the top of the sales ladder was, at times, challenging. However, the friends and relationships he cultivated during his climb are the same people keeping him at the top of his game today. He taught me that interpersonal, soft skills and customer service need to be synonymous. This is a precious lesson I share in all my classes.

Here's another one:

In 1982, after successfully graduating with a degree in theater and communications from Wagner College in Staten Island, New York, I was lost and felt hopeless. I experienced staggering amounts of difficulty trying to find a job outside of the acting world. My acting skills allowed me to excel and shine in all my job interviews, but in the end, everyone told me, *"Thanks, but no thanks!"* Why? Surprisingly, employers were not interested in hiring anyone with a college degree in theatrical arts. They believed that theatre people would quit the job as soon as an acting role came along. Therefore, I was too much of a "risk." If I had been aware of this information earlier, I would not have quit acting right after graduation due to my perceived lack of talent.

However, in late November of 1982, my luck changed for the better. I began working as a customer service rep at the Federal Home Loan Bank, on the 103rd floor of the World Trade Center in New York City. I mentioned this in chapter 5. It was my first real job after graduation, and I quickly decided to be the best rep they ever hired. I was grateful for the job and figured the best way to demonstrate my gratitude was to become an outstanding employee. After all, how difficult could it be? It was a simple customer service position, and my only objective was to assist the customers and treat them with respect so they'd continually do business with us. I was thrilled because the job entailed only phone work. I believed that phone work was much more comfortable and less stressful than working face to face with customers.

Gratefully, my enthusiasm and positive attitude were noticed quickly by my immediate supervisor. Quite soon, I received my first employee review and my very first pay raise. Wow! I was rich (or so I thought), only 21 years old, and already earning $10,150.00 per year! ($405.00 biweekly after taxes.)

My favorite customer was a very affluent man by the name of Mr. Meynard. He was the president of a bank in Rome, NY, and a powerful man in the industry. Although we never met face to face, we quickly became comrades even though we had a very uncomfortable first phone call. The first time he called my bank, I politely answered the phone, and he abruptly asked, *"How old are you? You sound very young, and I need to speak with an experienced rep!"* Without hesitation, I quickly replied, *"I am new here, Mr. Meynard, but I'm thoroughly trained, and I'm sure I can help you with your request and provide the excellent service with which you are accustomed."* He must have appreciated my professionalism, so he explained his issue, and I quickly resolved it with irresistible enthusiasm.

Our friendship grew from there. Besides business, most of our conversations revolved around how much he enjoyed the tranquility in Rome, NY, and my complaining about how noisy and crowded New York City was. We made each other laugh and always had something positive to contribute to each other's day.

The best gift he ever gave to me was a very well written letter of commendation to my supervisor. He praised my professionalism, integrity, attitude, personality, and honesty. Mr. Meynard also recommended that I train the entire customer service department because their skills were not as adequate as mine. At that time, I had no desire to be a trainer, but his letter to my supervisor did earn me a promotion and another raise. I heartily thanked Mr. Meynard for sending my supervisor such an outstanding letter regarding my services. When I inquired as to why he felt compelled to write to my supervisor, he replied:

"Because John, dealing with you over the past year, always gave me the feeling that I had a friend on the inside, someone who could pull some strings and get things done when others couldn't."

I always remembered that compliment, and years later, it serves as a soft skill inspiration for this book. We were extremely loyal to each other. We had each other's back, and in many cases, if I became aware of a surfacing problem, I'd resolve it long before he became aware of it or called me for help. Long after I left the bank and began my seminar business, Mr. Meynard and I remained friends. Although Mr. Meynard was my favorite customer, I'm proud to say that I had the same professional relationship with over 90% of my clients and customers.

Think about it! Imagine how much more successful and prosperous your business can be by earning and maintaining clients with this type of unshakeable *loyalty*! As a rep, what would your customer satisfaction rates look like if you could create that type of euphoria over your services and products? The dictionary defines *"euphoric"* as a feeling of intense excitement and happiness. It explains *"loyal"* as giving or showing firm and constant support or allegiance to a person, institution, or business. In the end, it's all about utilizing your soft skills for building relationships. Customers prefer to do business with friends and prefer to remain loyal to companies that are loyal to them. Clients like to give their hard-earned money to businesses they trust.

Think of the immeasurable benefits you, your company, and your team would enjoy by mastering these soft skills.

Soft Skills Required to Be a Rep Successful

If you have a strong desire to own or to work in a service-centered industry, I'd like to be the first to tell you that I think you're out of your mind. Why would any sane person want to deal with crying, whining, complaining customers all day or for an entire career? On the other hand, if you have a strong desire to own or work in a service-centered industry, I'd also like to be the first to tell you that it can be one of the most rewarding and satisfying careers of a lifetime. Why? If you have the soft skills and personality to deal with crying, whining, complaining customers all day, it can be quite gratifying. I've always enjoyed the art and skill involved in converting an angry customer into a loyal fan. I've always viewed it as a game or sport. I used to keep a scorecard on my desk and measure how quickly and how many difficult people I could turn around in a single day. It made my day fun and helped the time pass very quickly.

I've been privileged to meet some of the most talented and highest-paid customer service reps in the industry. I have found them to be motivated, enthusiastic, personable, witty, and conscientious. They also have very high levels of productivity and always came to work with a smile. After spending so much time with so many service reps, I slowly became aware of four specific personality traits they all had in common. I believe these traits are keys to their success. If you are interviewing for any customer service or service-centered position, I know you'll find this information valuable. Let me share the personality traits with you:

First – They Genuinely Love People.

If an interviewer asks you why they should hire you as their customer service rep, enthusiastically answer that you love people. Then be prepared to back that claim up with a professional example. Loving people is a master key! If you don't love dealing with people, do not apply for any job where you're required to serve them. Truthfully, some employees are more productive if you lock them in a back room without any type of human interaction. These folks don't like dealing with people and should not be on the front line or connecting with customers in any way. Honestly, ask yourself, *"Do I love people and interpersonal interactions?"* If your answer is an enthusiastic "yes," then a customer service career could be a perfect fit for you.

Second - They Place Great Value in Serving Others.

If an interviewer asks what you like about serving others, answer that you enjoy making people happy and solving their problems. Inherent in the job title, "customer service" is the word "service." Many customers can be quite negative or angry, and these chronic personalities can take massive tolls on your physical and mental health. Providing QUALITY client service every day–all the time–can be fun and challenging, but is not always easy. A customer service rep needs to be a good actor or actress, which can be hard work. If you're having a bad day, you must learn to fake it. If you want to convince your customer that you're here to serve them, never sound or look like you're too busy to assist or that you're distracted. Therefore, if you place a high value on serving others, then a customer service job or career could be a perfect fit for you.

Third – They are Good Communicators.

Possessing good communication skills doesn't mean you need to memorize a dictionary or thesaurus and have a multi-million-dollar vocabulary, although that is impressive. All the reps I've trained were successful because they knew how to do their jobs and consistently communicated an authentic feeling of concern, friendliness, and compassion. Their demeanor was positive, and their body language was always congruent with what they were saying. Truthfully, these are the essential ingredients required for impressive communication skills. If you can project your love of people and desire to serve "within" your communication style, then a customer service job could be a perfect fit for you.

Fourth – They all Possess the Gift of Patience.

Patience is just as important as the previous three. If you want to be involved in a service-centered industry, you must have the gift of patience, and plenty of it. Patience is a crucial skill when dealing with clients and customers. Patience helps you communicate more effectively, listen better, think better, and resolve issues more successfully. Some of your clients will complain, some will speak very slowly, some very quickly. Some customers may have a dialect that is difficult to understand. Some will lie, and some will call you all through the day, every day. Patience is truly a virtue because it can help you rise above many of the customer service job's challenges.

Please read the questions below; they are a simple common sense approach to building human relations. And as we will discuss, human connections should always precede customer service.

As a review, here are the four questions for you:

1. Do I genuinely love people?   Yes   No

2. Do I place great value on serving others?   Yes   No

3. Am I a good communicator?   Yes   No

4. Do I have lots of patience?   Yes   No

If you can, without hesitation, enthusiastically answer "yes" to the above questions, then **WELCOME** to the customer service industry. Begin searching and applying for these jobs. You will enjoy a fulfilling career. You will enjoy a very nice salary, and you will be a great asset to any company. More importantly, at the end of every workday, you'll know you've made a difference in many customers' lives. Remember, every job or career you chose will involve variations of customer service.

Here are three great questions for you:

1. Are you aware that your customers can Google the same services you offer and find thousands of other businesses willing to meet their needs in only a few seconds?

2. Did you ever stop to think about how easy it is for your customers to "not" do business with you?

3. In the 80s, the vinyl record business crashed and burned overnight. Compact discs quickly replaced vinyl, even while its' ashes were still smoldering. Eventually, karma used "streaming" to deliver a final blow to CDs. Is it possible that your business could suffer the same fate?

It's terrifying to think about, but these are genuine threats alive and well in the business world. If you don't consistently exceed your client's needs, you and your business will be yesterday's news quicker than you can blink your eyes. In America, 96% of all new companies crash and burn in less than ten years.

"The # 1 reason behind this statistic is the inability to satisfy, connect, and bond with customers."

The following is a concept known as the chart of "Consumer Evolution." It offers insight into the type of consumers your business is attracting. It also gives you some insight into how well you are satisfying, connecting, and bonding with your customers. Let's check it out:

The 6 Level Consumer Evolution Chart

Level 1 = A Shopper

I define a shopper as someone who occasionally visits your establishment or website and rarely makes a purchase. (AKA "window shoppers" and "tire kickers.") Shoppers' unpredictability and inconsistency make it challenging to earn a living or keep a business afloat. They may also visit your business up to ten times before they purchase. However, if they do buy and appreciate the service experience you offer, they will evolve to level 2.

Level 2 = A Customer

A happy shopper usually evolves into what most businesses call a customer. Customers visit your establishment or website more frequently, and they typically make purchases. Levels 1 and 2 indicate mediocre or indifferent clientele, combined with inferior products, service, and low word of mouth. However, if they still like your products and appreciated the experience you offered, they will evolve to level 3.

Level 3 = A Regular

You're doing well if you notice your customers are evolving into regulars. These folks regularly visit your establishment or website and happily make purchases at each visit. If they do "face to face" business with you, you can easily recognize them, and you probably know each other by name, inside and outside of your establishment. If they continue to enjoy your products and appreciate the experience you offered, they will evolve to level 4.

Level 4 = A Client

Another name for a level 4 client is a "satisfied customer." Level 4 can be risky and misleading at times. It's a level most companies strive to achieve, and when they have a lot of satisfied customers, they believe they've done enough, and their job is complete. As long as the customers are satisfied, you'd think you're are doing a great job. Right? Wrong!

The fact is that satisfied customers will only do business with you until someone else satisfies them better. Why? Because at level 4, there is NO LOYALTY. Again, they will do business with you **only** until someone else better serves them. Meaning, they are still shopping around and looking for deals elsewhere. The internet makes this extremely simple to do.

Ask any smart business owner if they would rather have shoppers or customers? They'll say, customers. Ask any intelligent business owner if they would rather have customers or regulars? They will say, regulars.

Ask any intelligent business owner if they would rather have regulars or clients. They will say, clients.

Levels 3 and 4 indicate that your products and service have value. But, level 4 does not guarantee client loyalty or allegiance. However, if they still like your products and appreciated the experience you offered, with some time, you can lead them to the 2nd most valued level of all - level 5.

Level 5 = A Raving Fan

Ask any intelligent business owner if they would rather have clients or raving fans? They will say, RAVING FANS!

Level 5 indicates you have earned their utmost trust and loyalty. Raving fans will **only** do business with you. If asked, they will always recommend your services and bring you referrals. If asked, they will write positive Google reviews for you. Research also indicates that a raving fan is worth about 10-15 times their initial investment. You can help your clients evolve to level 5 by consistently providing them with greater value, experiences, service, and friendship than they have received elsewhere.

As you can see, it doesn't make financial sense to have level 4 as your ultimate goal. Level 5 raving fans will keep you employed for a very long time. As a rep, the more customers you can convert into raving fans, the more value you will hold in your career or job.

Level 6 = An Apostle

Level 6 is when you convert a raving fan into an "apostle." Level 6 is the crest, the pinnacle, the top of the mountain, the zenith, and the apex level. Levels 5 and 6 are the target for which every business must strive. It's a vital sign you're providing an expectation shattering experience, and your product or service is superior. Converting a raving fan into an apostle takes time, and you must work hard to earn this level. It is the most significant level of all and the "holy grail" for any business or rep. We call them apostles because they continually "spread the word" and "sing your praises," even if you **DO NOT** ask them to do so. Through the power of "word of mouth," they do all your advertising for you and become your living, breathing billboards. They carry your business card in their wallet at all times. Also, they are worth up to 20 times their original investment. Truthfully, apostles can sell your services better than the owner, president, or CEO. They will also promote your business better than your most expensive marketing campaign. With level 2 customers, you'll scarcely earn a living, but with level 6 apostles, you'll create a prosperous, thriving, booming business, and their loyalty is boundless. Another exciting fact is that when apostles refer new customers, those newbie's already like and trust you. Their loyalty does not need to be earned because their commitment to you is already built-in, pre-established, and intact since the referral came from an apostle.

"Other than exceptional employees, level 6 apostles are the most valuable assets any company can acquire. Once you find one, treat them better than gold and never let them go."

If your patrons are at levels 1, 2, 3, or 4 and you're interested in taking them to levels 5 and 6, this chapter will describe the required principles to help you and your company achieve that objective. However, I do want to be transparent with you. I do not believe it to be possible to convert all your clients into level 6 euphoric apostles, simply because some people are never satisfied, no matter how excellent your products and services may be. However, I do believe in time, you can convert many of them. I've had a few toxic clients whom I happily re-directed to my competition. I simply did not want to deal with their negative attitudes. I didn't appreciate how they treated my team, and more importantly, I was feeling spiteful towards this competitor and seeking vengeance.

Converting Your Customers into Euphoric Apostles!

I want to share "The 13 Ultimate Objectives of Every Client Interaction." They will serve as an essential guideline or measuring post, helping you serve your customers at the highest possible levels. They are the fastest path to converting apostles to your business. If you are applying for a sales, hospitality, or service rep position, you'll demonstrate high levels of competency and expertise by adhering to and consistently delivering the following objectives. These are proven soft skills for climbing the ladder, advancing your career, and earning a higher salary. I recommend you place a copy of these objectives in a highly visible place in your work area. Use them as a reminder and "check-off" list. After each customer interaction, ask yourself the following questions:

The 13 Ultimate Objectives of Every Client Interaction

1. Did I help the customer feel **WELCOME?**
    - Did you ever walk into an establishment and were improperly greeted or not greeted at all?

- Did an employee behind a counter ever roll their eyes as you walked in the door?
- Was an employee on a personal call and refused to hang up while you were waiting for service?
- Did a customer service rep ever place you on hold, yet you overheard them speaking negatively about you?
- Did you ever visit that business again? I hope not!

If your customers do not feel welcome, safe, and secure when they walk through your door, they will never do business with you again. Companies dealing with the above issues need to replace or re-train their frontline and then train all new-hires in the art of soft skills. Soft skills must be a significant focus of your onboarding processes.

"The protocol for resolving this issue remember to smile."

The # 1 way to make a customer feel welcome is to greet them with a happy, sincere smile. A smile is powerful in person and over the phone. Two old classic expressions say:

"Your customer can hear your face through the phone."

"Smile when ya dial."

I recommend placing a small sign or sticker on or near your phone, reminding you to smile brightly. I recently taught a seminar at a call center in Texas, and they painted a large sign on the wall that said, *"Smile, please; we need apostles!"* It served as a potent reminder.

Did you ever think about placing a small mirror on your desk, so you can observe your face as you speak to your customers on the phone? It may sound strange and make you feel a little uncomfortable initially, but it works. I instruct all my classes to use this mirror technique, and most of them begin to improve their telephone interactions in about a day. The ability to see your face during a customer interaction can be quite transforming. We'll talk more specifically about soft skills telephone interactions in chapter 9.

Here are several often-over-looked reasons to smile with an attitude of gratitude:

- Your customers are paying your bills.
- Your customers are putting food on your table.
- Your customers are supporting your family.
- Your customers are helping to pay for your medical insurance.
- Your customers are paying your rent or mortgage.
- Your customers are helping pay for your vacation.

The list is truly endless! Aren't those great reasons to afford all your customers a smile? Remember, the direction of your day always goes in the direction that the corners of your mouth point.

2. Did I help my customer feel **UNDERSTOOD?**

From everyday interactions to global conflicts, we've hit rock-bottom in our levels of compassion, and it's a shame. In his landmark book, *"The 7 Habits of Highly Effective People,"* Stephen Covey states, *"We must first seek to understand before being understood."* You can easily accomplish this by demonstrating sincere empathy.

An essential step in developing empathy is to practice being a better listener. Customers appreciate an empathetic customer service rep because it demonstrates that you have the ability and skills to put yourself in their shoes. Empathy is a crucial skill to master, especially if a client becomes unhappy or angry. Empathy can turn a negative client into a positive one. More importantly, empathy can convert level 4 clients into level 6 apostles. Empathy is also an essential trait for you to project at an interview.

3. Did I help my customer to feel **IMPORTANT?**

Think about it. Don't you like to feel important when you do business with other companies? It makes you feel good, and it builds deep rapport.

"In my experience, the perfect way to help a client feel important is to remember and use their name."

Think of a time when someone you had met only once before greeted you the next time you met by name. Were you impressed? Didn't it feel good? When people remember your name, it builds your self-esteem. Customers feel more valued and respected when we remember their names. They feel more engaged in a conversation when we use their name. When you address a customer by name, it shows you see that person as an individual. When you remember their name, it shows your interest and respect, and it's an essential, impressive soft skill.

Remembering someone's name can make a difference in how that person feels about you. *"A person's name is to him or her the sweetest and most important sound in any language,"* writes Dale Carnegie in his classic book, *"How to Win Friends and Influence People."*

My family and I visit the Shanghai Express Chinese Restaurant in Marton, NJ, several times a month. It's about a half-mile from our home. The food is excellent, but the service and the owner are simply outstanding. The owner's name is Ted, and his soft skills are impeccable. Ted always happily greets everyone at the door. He always smiles, frequently has something funny to say, and most of all, he remembers everyone's name. The first time the family and I ate dinner at his restaurant, Ted introduced himself and asked us our names. He made us feel **comfortable, welcome,** and **important**. I felt as if I came home to a place I've never been to before. The food was excellent, and we were impressed. Life got busy for us after that first meal, and we did not visit Ted and his restaurant for about two months. Although Ted only met us once, when we revisited his restaurant, he remembered everyone's name and what we ordered two months earlier. We were amazed! He has some of the most exceptional interpersonal skills I've ever witnessed, and we are his apostles. I'm such a devoted apostle, I'm writing about him in this book. Recently, I took a moment to figure out some math: Our average bill is $85, and we've been eating there at least twice a month for about ten years. That means Ted's excellent customer service skills, remarkable memory, and apostle conversion ability earned him approximately $20,400.00 just from our family. That's a good return on investment for simply remembering names and serving great food. What do you think? Wow!

Tips for Remembering Names

It's a fact that people love their names, and we can create quick rapport when remembering names.

Step 1 - If you have difficulty with your memory, inconspicuously write the name down where you can quickly reference it. Do the same if you're speaking to customers on the phone. Write it down! Write it down!

Step 2 – After someone introduces themselves to you, it can be beneficial to repeat their name during the conversation subtly. The repetition can help improve your recall. Professional business etiquette states that it's helpful to use your customer's name at least twice over the phone or in person. Mounting evidence confirms that using an angry customer's name during a negative interaction helps calm that person and relieves their anxiety. This gives you greater control for peacefully and rapidly resolving the issue.

Step 3 – As a memory hook, try creating a mental picture of the person's name. For example, do you know someone who has the same name? Does their name rhyme with something? Does their name have a melodic element to it? Does the name remind you of something or someone?

Another valuable tool to help customers feel important is to thank them for doing business with you. Take a moment to reflect on the many reasons that you appreciate your customer. It's even more effective if you make a list and review it often, as I did a few pages back. A list can remind you of some things we usually take for granted in our customers. I mentioned I call this skill serving customers with an "attitude of gratitude." Let's review a few more:

- *"Thank you for paying my salary."*
- *"Thank you for helping me pay my mortgage."*
- *"Thank you for helping me put food on my table."*
- *"Thank you for my new car."*

- *"I appreciate you giving me the privilege of serving you."*
- *"I feel lucky, honored, and blessed to have a job at all."*
- *"Thank you for choosing me to do your business with."*

As a footnote, there is mounting medical and psychological evidence stating that people who continually express their gratitude are: healthier, more successful, have more friends, have better relationships, have more energy, and sleep better than those who do not. Consider it.

4. Did I help my customer feel **COMFORTABLE?**

The most crucial point to focus on here is that they feel comfortable deciding to do business with you. A negative example of this could be buyer's remorse. However, there is not much you need to do or be concerned with as far as this point is related. If you have completely satisfied or exceeded at points 1, 2, and 3, their comfort will automatically fall into a positive place. It's merely a natural and predictable progression.

5. Did I build **RAPPORT?**

We discussed rapport in chapter 3, and I recommend you review it. But, remember that rapport is the most critical ingredient required for building relationships with your customers. It is the bridge that leads to open communication and interpersonal skills. Rapport is power!

6. Was I **FRIENDLY?**

- Did I smile?
- Did I greet them warmly?
- Did I demonstrate empathy?
- Did I remember their name?
- Was I helpful and gracious?

7. Was I **COMPETENT**?

The dictionary defines competence as having the necessary ability, knowledge, or skill to do something successfully. Your competency level distinguishes you from your competition.

8. Was I **POSITIVE**?

In chapter 4, we defined "attitude" as to how you project your mood to others. Positivity is contagious and highly promotable. What kind of attitude do you project at an interview? What kind of attitude do you project to your customers or co-workers?

- Are you happy to see them when they walk through the door?
- Do you sincerely ask how they are and actively listen for a response?
- Are you grateful for their business?
- Do you appreciate the fact that your customer pays your bills?
- Do you engage in meaningful communication?
- Are you good a "small talk?" (A critical soft skill.)
- Do you say "thank you" to your customers?

Crispin Cleaners is a fantastic dry-cleaning establishment located very close to our home. The people working there are some of the most friendly and positive people with whom I've ever done business. On my first visit to this establishment, I had my then one-year-old daughter, Erica, with me. The very personable ladies behind the counter insisted that they take a picture of Erica. They wanted to hang it on their wall for all their customers to see. Being a very proud and flattered dad, I happily agreed. One week later, my daughter's picture was hanging on their wall for all to see. This simple act touched me so profoundly that I have been sending them referrals and business ever since. Today, they have dozens of other baby pictures hanging on their walls. I estimate that I have spent over $5000.00 at this establishment over the years. That's quite a return on their money, considering the original picture probably cost them less than ten cents. Of course, they provide excellent customer service, yet their attention and positive attitude to my daughter turned me into a loyal apostle.

9. Was I **TIMELY?**

In the business world, there are only two types of timeliness:

"Early" or "On time!"

Early ranks as the all-time favorite. You must deliver on your promises if you want to convert raving fans and apostles. I know this is common sense, but sometimes common sense is not so common. Don't make promises, assure delivery, or guarantee an outcome unless you are 100% sure you can pull it off. One of my favorite strategies is to promise delivery a little later than I expect it. In this manner, if a customer's order comes in on time, I can deliver earlier than expected and smell like a rose. If it comes in late, I have a fudge factor so I can deliver on time.

"I firmly believe that reliability is a much more effective soft skill approach than far-out promises."

My wife recently needed a prescription filled from our local pharmacy. They promised us it would be ready for pick-up at 1 pm. However, it wasn't ready when I arrived. They apologized and asked if I could come back in an hour. I returned at 2 pm, and the prescription was still not ready. This went on until 4 pm. They had all kinds of excuses for their blunders, yet they still did not have the script prepared even after all their apologizing. I told them I would be busy for the next few hours and would not return until 7 pm. I was extremely frustrated and exhausted from running back and forth to the pharmacy. At about 4:30 pm that same afternoon (about 30 minutes later), there was a knock on our door. Much to my surprise and delight, one of the pharmacists was standing on my porch with the medicine in his hand. I jokingly asked, *"Since when do you guys deliver?"* He replied, *"We don't deliver; we're making this rare exception for you because we gave you such poor service and hope you'll forgive us."* But wait; there's more! He also gave us a $20 gift certificate to reimburse me for the gas I used driving back and forth earlier that afternoon. I happily thanked him, forgave him, and we still do business with that pharmacy. The pharmacist now knows my name, pleasantly greets me every time he sees me, and we've become very friendly. Since that incident, I have referred about ten people to that establishment. Isn't it amazing how easy it is to please a customer if you are willing to go that extra mile for them?

Should you ever accidentally break your word when it comes to timeliness, be sure you quickly and sincerely utilize the four steps to a professional apology, as we discussed earlier.

10. Did I demonstrate EFFICIENCY & EFFECTIVENESS?

Companies often speak about employee effectiveness and efficiency when brainstorming strategies to improve productivity. While they sound similar, there is a dramatic difference between these two terms, and your customers expect both from your company. The differences are:

"Efficient" people do things right.

"Effective" people do the right thing.

Here's an interesting example. Imagine walking into a small crowded barbershop with a 90-minute waiting period. There are only two barbers on the job. One barber is busy sweeping excess hair off the floor, while the other barber is busy cutting hair.

My question to you is which barber is efficient and which is effective?

The answer is the barber sweeping the floor is efficient because he is doing things right. However, the barber cutting hair is effective simply because he is doing what absolutely needs to be done at that very moment. When you have a large crowd of customers waiting for service, the effective thing is to serve them first; sweeping the floor can wait. An effective employee produces at a high level, while an efficient employee simply produces. If you desire a management position, be on the look-out for reps performing efficiently when effectiveness is warranted. Simultaneously, be on the look-out for typically effective team members only functioning at an efficient level. By combining effectiveness with efficiency, you can convert apostles faster and with fewer resources.

11. Was I HONEST?

I define honesty as the total and complete absence of deceit. Although lately, it seems some corporate conglomerates have forgotten, *"Honesty is still the best policy."* As part of our soft skills training, we must accept full responsibility for our errors and quickly admit our mistakes. If possible, we should acknowledge our mistakes before our customer brings them to our attention. As a friend to your customer, you must be accountable for all that you do. Accountability is a sure sign to your customer that they are dealing with a professional and can help you build rapport. In many cases, rapport with your client can be so deep that they overlook errors and easily forgive your mistakes. This is especially true when dealing with apostles.

I have never exaggerated or lied to a customer. If I made a mistake or screwed something up, I always told them ahead of time. I always had a fear that they already knew what happened and were just testing my integrity. If that were true, I'd be caught in a lie and look like an even bigger idiot. You cannot attain level 6 apostles if you're a liar. When I reflect on the disgusting fraud Volkswagen pulled on their customers by altering the emission tests on some of their vehicles, or how the banking industry drained customers of their life savings, I'm amazed they are still in business. Perhaps they were relying on the fact that the public has a short memory. I live by the motto, *"If I lie, they won't buy!"* As a footnote, apostles have great memories, or they wouldn't be apostles.

12. Did I treat the customer like a **VIP**?

Mr. Angelo Salandra, a friend of mine, is the Founder and President of the very successful Quality Copy in Philadelphia. While vacationing recently, he received a frantic phone call from a client who needed 25 sets of 405 originals to settle a significant court case. The copies had to be collated, bound, and delivered to the courthouse by morning. Mr. Salandra cut his vacation short, completed the job, and personally delivered the copies to the courthouse. His client was genuinely grateful and appreciative. In this instance, I believe Angelo went beyond the call of duty, convincing his client that he is a VIP. And it worked! He became a valued apostle.

13. Was I **PROFESSIONAL**?

There is not much you need to do or be anxious about as far as this point is concerned. If you have completely satisfied or exceeded objectives 1-12, your customer will automatically recognize your professionalism. All 12 objectives encapsulate the art of professionalism. It's merely a natural and predictable progression. As a reminder after every client interaction, it would be beneficial to ask yourself:

The 13 Ultimate Objectives of Every Client Interaction (Review)

1. Did I help my customer feel **WELCOME?**

2. Did I help my customer feel **UNDERSTOOD?**

3. Did I help my customer feel **IMPORTANT?**

4. Did I help my customer feel **COMFORTABLE?**

5. Did I create **RAPPORT?**

6. Was I **FRIENDLY?**

7. Was I **COMPETENT?**

8. Was I **POSITIVE?**

9. Was I **TIMELY?**

10. Did I demonstrate **EFFICIENCY & EFFECTIVENESS?**

11. Was I **HONEST?**

12. Did I treat my customer as a **VIP?**

13. Was I **PROFESSIONAL?**

If you answered "yes," to all thirteen questions, then you're well on your way to apostle conversion. You're going to increase your value in the job market, and you're going to be an indispensable employee. If you answered "no," to any or all the questions, it's critical to begin polishing those soft skills and implementing them immediately.

Earlier I also recommended making copies of these objectives and placing them in strategic locations throughout your office for easy viewing. Let them serve as a ringing reminder that we must be serving our customers at the highest levels possible, all the time.

What about Angry Customers?

Can I build rapport with angry or unhappy customers? What if they barge into my workplace like Satan with a score to settle? What if they are screaming and yelling? What if their face is red hot, their blood pressure is boiling, and you can see their fangs? Yes, you can!

At some point in your career, I'm sure you've had the pleasure of dealing with angry customers. It's no secret that dealing with the public can be a very challenging job. Unhappy or dissatisfied customers can ruin your entire day and create large amounts of unnecessary stress. They storm into your place of business, or on the phone, like an angry, miserable bear with constipation. In most instances, despite your best efforts, some customers simply want to complain, scream, and vent.

Unfortunately, there is no magic formula to please every single person all the time. While transforming an angry customer into a happy one can be challenging, it is possible. The more negative people you deal with, the more you will polish your soft skills. Please allow me to repeat something we mentioned earlier – *"Negative customers pay our salary as well as positive customers."*

However, there are many things you can do to maintain an upbeat and positive attitude of gratitude while you're swimming in a sea of negativity. I believe that the employee who can keep their mouth closed is the employee who stays employed. The following are more soft skill ideas that have been helpful for me when resolving customer issues and building rapport:

1. Take the customer off the floor quickly. Especially if the blow-out is happening where other customers can hear or observe the incident. Escort the irate to a location where your other customers cannot hear or video what's happening. That situation can create a more substantial, unnecessary disturbance. Once you have the customer in a private area, let them vent and complain as much as they want, and don't interrupt them. Always have a witness present.

2. Never, ever interrupt an irate! It's important to remember that sometimes people just want to be heard. They need someone to listen to them, and if you interrupt while they're venting, it may create more anger. It is also unprofessional and ineffective to say, *"I won't help you unless you're nice."* Instead, let them vent until they run out of steam, and this will give you the upper hand. Although it may not always be pleasant, as a rep, that is your job. While they are venting, I always recommend that you imagine they are a loved one or an exceptional friend. A perception shift like that can help keep you calm. Perhaps you can visualize a massive $ stamped on their forehead. That image will help you remember that your customer is paying your bills and feeding your family, and the outcome of this interaction may or may not cost you your job. Remember, a happy customer equals your paycheck. These simple mind shifts can help you remain calm in highly charged situations. Your job is **NOT** to win an argument with a customer. Your job is to make them happy and keep them loyal, so you continue getting paid.

3. Lower your voice. After the customer has vented and it's your turn to speak, you will find it very beneficial if you lower your voice. Sarcasm, scolding, or being the louder voice are poor strategies with a shallow success rate. After dropping your voice, always use an even, conversational tone to help keep your customer relaxed. I have found that utilizing "silence" often can also be a powerful soft skill tool in building rapport. Again, sometimes customers just want to be heard and need someone to listen. Sometimes people just need to vent. Remember, a closed mouth gathers no feet.

4. Use their name. Remember, the sweetest sound to any person's ear is the sound of their name. Research indicates that saying "Yes, sir" and "Yes, miss," while polite, are not as effective as using your customer's actual name. In any argument, conflict, or problem-solving process, you will always maintain the upper hand and control if you speak the person's name occasionally.

5. Demonstrate your empathy. We have already spoken about the power of empathy. In other words, you are placing yourself in their shoes. However, please do not allow yourself to get drawn into their anger or begin to take their negativity personally. You must remain detached from their personality and keep your focus on the issue and solution. The more you focus on your angry customer's personality, the more likely it will be for you to lose your cool. The more you focus on a positive outcome, it's less likely you'll be distracted by their negativity. Also, avoid company jargon that will make your customer feel confused. Company jargon and technical talk can quickly breach rapport, causing your customer to feel isolated or out of the loop.

6. Body Language. Use your body language and voice to indicate your sincere willingness to resolve the problem or issue. Use your body language and voice to demonstrate your high level of self-confidence and patience. By projecting a desire to help and a professional aura of confidence, you can more easily de-escalate a negative situation creating rapport. Smiling, when appropriate, is a beautiful rapport builder. You can double the effectiveness of your smile by maintaining an open posture. Opening and relaxing your posture is a key strategy, helping lower your customer's defenses, leading to a speedier resolution. A relaxed posture means your hands must be in full view at all times, never in your pocket or behind your back. A "slight forward lean" is also a powerful body language gesture. It signals that you're concerned, empathetic, and listening intently. Remember, your main goal is to build rapport-- not resistance.

7. Take notes. Listen fully and take notes if appropriate, especially if your customer is aggressively ranting. The simple act of witnessing your note-taking will cause your customer to slow down and speak more amicably while you catch up with your much slower note-taking.

If you're dealing with an upset customer on the phone, who is babbling uncontrollably, calmly and politely say to them, *"Jessica, to resolve this issue and give you the best service possible, I'm trying to write down every word you say. With your permission, may I ask you to slow down a bit?"* Then, be sure to thank them when they do. However, please remember that none of this is useful unless you "sound sincere." (Notice I mentioned her name in the request.)

8. Use appropriate humor. I'm sure you've used humor in your life to turn angry people around. I am a firm believer that if appropriately used, humor can move mountains. If you deliver humor well and have great timing, humor builds rapport by lowering people's defenses. It's a fantastic tool for getting people to relax. However, take caution. Humor can brutally backfire if you have not perfected the skill. Take caution if using humor in emails. Humorous emails or jokes usually do not translate well, and what you think is funny, someone else may find offensive. When in doubt, leave it out.

9. Optimistic statements. Making optimistic statements is just as effective as humor if done correctly. Try to make a sincere, optimistic statement whenever possible. Statements such as:

"We can work this out for you!"

"I'm sure this issue will never happen again."

"I have lots of experience dealing with this kind of concern."

"Rather than telling you what I can't do, allow me to tell you what I can do for you."

Optimistic statements and this type of positive approach will help your customer appreciate your confidence levels and realize you've got their back. It can also help your customer see the light at the end of the tunnel.

10. Challenge yourself to find something to like about every customer. While this may seem complicated, if you try hard enough, you can find something to like about everyone, even if it's the color of their tie. During an angry customer encounter, practice keeping your focus **on the 5%** you like about them and your **focus off the 95%** you dislike.

Bonus Tips

Another idea is to show your customer how much you value their opinion by continually asking them for feedback. Remember, excellent service is in the eye of the beholder. Your measurement of quality service might not be what your customer believes it to be. 80% of companies believe they deliver "superior" customer service. Sadly, only 8% of their customers think these same companies provide "superior" service. The scariest fact is that most dissatisfied customers do not complain. They simply switch over to the competition leaving you flat and clueless. A typical business hears from only 4% of its unhappy customers, and it takes twelve positive experiences to make up for one unresolved, negative experience. So, by asking for feedback, you can meet your customer's needs each time, every time. Therefore, the angry, complaining customer is just as valuable to a business as a satisfied customer. Why? Because they are usually willing to give you another chance if you satisfactorily resolve their issue.

In my seminars, I teach managers and reps to view all feedback as a "gift." When your customer offers you feedback or criticism, they provide you with a recipe for how they want you to serve them. It is also an unconscious clue that they are willing to do business with you again if you make the required changes. One of the surest marks of good character is our ability to accept personal criticism without feeling malice to the one who gives it. So, thank your client for all their feedback, then take this "gift in disguise" and run with it. Criticism should always leave us feeling as if we've been helped.

"When we view feedback as a gift, we can be saved by criticism instead of ruined by praise."

What if the Customer is Wrong?

I'm frequently asked, *"How do I respond if my customer is wrong; what is the proper approach?"* The phrase *"The customer is always right"* was initially coined in 1909 by Harry Gordon Selfridge, the founder of Selfridge's department store in London. The slogan is used by businesses to convince customers that they will receive excellent service *and* persuade employees to provide such service.

"In 1909, that slogan worked very effectively. However, in today's business climate, the customer is always right-- is <u>wrong</u>."

Why? The slogan gives abrasive customers the advantage, and they'll begin to demand almost everything and anything. Some customers will take complete advantage and suck you dry. If you consistently make your customers right, you'll be out of business in the blink of an eye. The truth is that many times the customer is just plain wrong! Yet this fact should in no way disrupt the incredible experience you must deliver. Since your customer is the reason you have a job, you'll want to avoid squabbling or bickering with them. Do not rub their noses in it. You will not score any points by proving your customers wrong or by making them feel dim-witted. Your job is not to show them why they are wrong and why you are right. Your job is not to win an argument with your clients. If you know and can prove your customer is wrong, your only response must be to "save their face." Saying things such as, *"It could happen to anyone."* Or, *"I've made the same mistake many times"* can be a real rapport builder.

The words you choose in a situation such as this can destroy or repair a client's perception of who you are. Your words can also help you make deep emotional connections with your customers. So, choose your words and how you convey them very carefully. Remember, your job is not to win fights but to convert raving fans and apostles. Your customer may be wrong, but the rep with soft skills allows them to be wrong while "maintaining their dignity." Remember, if you fight or argue with a customer and win, you still lose. Such losses are reflected in your paycheck and bottom-line eventually.

"Our customers might not always be right, but they are always our customers."

Many years ago, I was an instructor for The Silva Method of Mind Development. It was a fantastic seminar. The training teaches a profound philosophy. It's a simple yet useful tool to remind us about how we must treat each other. I consistently try to make this the focal point of all my interactions and business affairs. The Silva philosophy is:

"Depending on their ages, remember to continually treat everyone you meet as you would treat your mother or father, brother or sister, son or daughter."

That has always been my life's mission and should be the focal point of all human relations. It will give you the mark of distinction, and your fans or apostles will remain loyal to you and your company.

Ask yourself honestly, *"How would I like my family member to be treated if they were in this business/customer relationship?"* This mindset is critical if your goal is to keep your customers for a lifetime. Remember, the moment you fumble a customer, your competition will quickly recover them.

A Professional Apology

We discussed these steps in chapter 3, and I promised you we would revisit them in detail. They are worth repeating because repetition is the mother of learning. As a review, business etiquette states that there are four steps to a professional apology. The steps are as follows:

First – Say, *"I'm sorry."* If possible, admit mistakes, errors, or blunders before your customer becomes aware of them. You'll find this to be an excellent way to build trusting, loyal relationships.

Second – Ask for forgiveness. Ask, *"Please forgive me?"* This is a crucial and often-overlooked step in our society. Most people believe that saying, *"I'm sorry"* is enough; it's not! You must hear your client say that they are *"going to let you slide,"* or *"it's water under the bridge,"* or *"don't worry about it,"* or *"it could happen to anyone."* This is your proof that they are ready and willing to move on and maintain the relationship.

Third – Honestly and sincerely say, *"It will never happen again,"* then it's your job to make sure that it doesn't. Under normal circumstances, this is where a professional apology would end. You only need these three steps. However, under very special or unique situations, you should employ the fourth step.

Fourth – Ask, *"Can I make it up to you?"* This step is a last resort, and whether you utilize it truly depends upon how much egg you have on your face. If you made a small, simple error, the first three steps would be sufficient. However, if you have committed a colossal blunder, have this fourth step in your arsenal ready to go.

Your customers don't expect perfection from you, although it may appear that way. All they desire is for you to be honest, trustworthy, and if a problem arises, they want you to fix it speedily. The most critical ingredient to help you stand out from the competition is how quickly and effectively you can resolve issues. That's an important point; remember it.

The L.A.S.T Approach

The L.A.S.T Approach is a powerful acronym designed to help you remember the most critical steps for creating an expectation-shattering experience for your customers. Some of the largest and most influential companies in our country use this method. I recommend you memorize it and use it as an answer to the interview question, *"How do you deal with difficult customers?"*

L = Listen – As you read through this process, you will notice that a fine-line runs through them, keeping them connected. The steps follow each other sequentially because you can't do one without the other. Listening is the first step because you can't help your customer until you understand their issue. Listening is a beautiful rapport builder, and it demonstrates your **empathy**.

A = Apologize – Your next step after listening and totaling comprehending the issue is to offer a professional apology, as we have already discussed. A professional apology demonstrates your **compassion**.

S = Solve – Now, it's time to resolve the issue. The faster and more accurately you can solve your customer's problem, the more effective you will be. You will increase your value within the company. Effective, practical problem solving demonstrates your **competence**.

T – Thank – If I had to make a top 5 list of the essential soft skills, remembering to say "thank you" would be high on that list. Regardless of whether the interaction was positive or negative, saying thank you will demonstrate your **professionalism**.

Bill Gates once said, "Your most unhappy customers are your greatest source of learning."

The Customer Service Soft Skills Survival Kit

This book aims to share essential soft skill strategies so that you can land the job and, more importantly, keep it. It's crucial that in difficult situations, you maintain a calm, collected demeanor. The last thing you want is to get terminated because you lost your temper. Therefore, I'd like to take some time and share some unique customer service "survival tactics" with you. These tactics are time-tested and have been utilized successfully by many of the most productive service reps I've known. Listed below are six steps that you can apply throughout the day to maintain your composure in adverse situations. I know you'll find them useful, and please, share them with friends or co-workers.

Survival Tip # 1. Skip the news before work.

How you spend the first couple of minutes of your day usually predicts how the rest of the day will unfold. Therefore, skip the news if possible. The news is always full of negativity. Mental health research states that exposing ourselves to any type of negativity at the start of our day can cause a 42% drop in our analytical skills. That's not good! It's always better to listen to pleasant, relaxing music or motivational content as you begin your day. These will fill your mind with the required positive motivation to help you tackle any problem or situation.

You can transform your car into a university on wheels by listening to some educational material to further your career. I do both, depending on my mood. Sometimes I listen to educational or motivational material, and sometimes I listen to some of my favorite music. Music has been a significant part of my life since I was a very young child. Good music lifts my spirit, heals my soul, and uplifts my mood. Two of my all-time favorite albums are the "Monkee's" debut album; I believe my parents purchased it for me when I was five years old. The 2nd is "Smile" by the Beach Boys. (This should give you an idea of how old I am.) Both albums are in my car, and I've listened to them each about a million times. It must help because I'm always productive on the job and in a good mood.

Survival Tip # 2. Use affirmations to support yourself.

Although we discussed affirmations in chapter two, I believe the information is worth reviewing. Repeating positive affirmations has become a valuable tool in the workplace and the clinical and medical fields. Like listening to motivational content, affirmations will fill your mind with positive messages to effectively tackle any problem, person, or situation. Affirmations help keep your mind focused on positive outcomes rather than the negative situation at hand. You can write a few on some sticky notes and hang them on your desk where you can see them. Here are some of my favorites:

* "I'm doing the best I can!"

* "I am a winner!"

* "I trust myself!"

* "I can handle any challenge!"

* "I like myself!"

* *"I deserve this job!"*

I also have another favorite hanging on my desk, taking priority over my other affirmations; let me explain. Did you know that a large percentage of American employees leave the office at the end of each day with a large assortment of headaches, migraines, eye strain, and anxiety? It's true! It seems that stress plays a significant role in how you will feel at quitting time. Besides the typical deadlines, meetings, angry customers, computer crashes, and other hassles occurring on the job, it seems another culprit contributes to how we feel at the end of the day.

As work stress accumulates, the body tends to breathe less, or at least our breathing becomes very shallow. When your body is deprived of oxygen, it can cause all kinds of issues, not to mention escalating our stress and agitation levels.

So, what's the solution? It's very simple!

"Hang a small sign on your desk reminding you to take a deep breath."

After that, anytime you see that sign, it will ring an internal bell and prompt you to take a nice, slow deep breath. People attending my training tell me that this simple idea has given them more energy, made them calmer, lowered blood pressure, and helped relieve pain associated with sitting in front of a computer all day. Wow, what great benefits and survival tools! Many people report a large increase in their deep breathing, from ten to twelve and even fifteen extra deep breaths daily. What a fantastic improvement simply because you hung a reminder sign on your desk. You'll also be amazed at how many of your co-workers will follow in your footsteps after they realize the significant benefits.

Survival Tip # 3. Always reward yourself for a job well done.

Sadly, this critical point is often overlooked. I've witnessed thousands of teams and reps quickly jump from one large, complicated project to the next, without ever once stepping back and admiring the tremendous job they've done. This must stop, or you can't survive. Imagine painting a room, writing a song, or planting a garden and never taking the time to enjoy your handiwork. When you've had a successful day, it's important to pat yourself on the back. After each project or team activity, reward yourself. You deserve it--- don't you? After a tough week or month, spend more time with family or friends. Go out for dinner or get a massage. Sleep late or take a long nap. These are very nice ways to demonstrate self-appreciation.

Survival Tip # 4. Keep a Praise File of thank you letters and every compliment you receive and review it often.

If you happen to receive thank you notes, emails, or accolades from customers, a "Praise File" is a beautiful idea. Anytime you receive a letter of appreciation from a customer, always make three copies:

- Place one in your human resources file.
- Take the second home and save it should you need a reference for another job.
- Keep the third in your praise file at your office desk.

You can review it during a tough week, and it can serve as a "pick-me-up." Simply take out the letters and read a few.

I'm incredibly grateful to have a praise file that is overflowing, starting with my first fan letter from Mr. Meynard. Sometimes it's important to remind ourselves that we are good, hard-working people. A praise file can help you feel better about yourself if you're feeling down. It will dramatically build your self-esteem, and it can remind you that you are appreciated, giving you the motivation to keep going.

In a recent seminar, a participant told the class a story of how a praise file helped her land a new job. She mentioned that she had been maintaining a praise file for over three years. She was, unfortunately, downsized and had to begin job hunting and going on interviews. She said that she had not been at an interview in several years and was quite nervous. Before her first interview, she began reading her fan mail from many satisfied customers throughout the years. She said it immediately brought back good, positive memories, giving her the energy and enthusiasm she needed to impress the interviewer. When the interviewer asked her if she had any references, she produced her praise file. The hiring manager was so impressed he offered her the job right on the spot. I love these success stories!

Survival Tip # 5. Avoid gossiping about negative customers, and avoid complainers, criticizers, and gossips in your office.

At a recent seminar, a participant told me that he wouldn't have anyone to speak with if he avoided all the complainers, criticizers, and gossip in the office. Regardless, this type of negativity fills your mind with destructive emotions that will cause your behavior and productivity to falter. You're also associating with a group that never rises higher than their current position.

"Birds of a feather flock together." Be an eagle!

Years ago, I saw actor Tom Cruise do an interview promoting his then-new movie, "Interview with a Vampire." When asked to summarize the movie plot in a short sentence, Tom said, *"It's about a vampire trying to find a hunting partner."* I was very impressed with that. Did you notice how many negative vampires on your job are looking for more negative people to socialize with? It's as if they need a team of negative supporters to help prove and support their case. Gossiping about negative customers will only intensify your anger and negativity. Also, the gossip causes you to relive the negative experience as if it never ended. However, it will also attract the vampires lurking in the shadows. They will quickly gather around you to support your negative views and, like a vampire, suck you dry. This will cause your stress levels to rise and your productivity to falter. It's essential to master the skill of "letting the negativity go" as soon as the customer leaves your space or phone. If not, that customer and the vampires will own and control your power.

"You've sold your soul to the customer without making a profit!"

Survival Tip # 6. List 10 things you're grateful for in your personal or business life and review it often.

The truth is that working long hours, deadlines, stress, and anxiety can cause us to quickly forget about how lucky we are that we have a job at all. A "Gratitude List" is very similar to the praise file. A gratitude list can serve as a reminder as to why you've chosen your career. A gratitude list will remind you of the good things you have and pivot your focus from stressful to resourceful. Gratitude is not only the greatest of virtues but the parent of all the others. If you forget the language of gratitude, you can never be on speaking terms with happiness. Therefore, if you can't be grateful for what you have, at least be grateful for what you've escaped.

Sometimes we need to be reminded about how good things indeed are, or at least that things are not as bad as we think. To help guide you and offer you a point of reference, here is the Top 10 Gratitude List that hangs by my desk. If you're involved in a very stressful career, review your gratitude list often.

1. I'm grateful for an easy commute and to work close to home.

2. I'm grateful for the amazing people I train and my co-workers.

3. I'm grateful for free, easy close to the door parking.

4. I'm grateful to work in a heated & air-conditioned environment.

5. I'm grateful to have a refrigerator and microwave close to my desk.

6. I'm grateful for my paycheck and benefits.

7. I'm grateful to be doing what I love.

8. I'm grateful that I have a comfortable chair & desk.

9. I'm grateful that the bathroom is close to my desk and rarely occupied.

10. I'm grateful to be able to dress casually.

I read this gratitude list almost daily; it centers and realigns me. More importantly, when the daily stressors pile up, it helps me to relax. It reminds me that there are positive things on which to focus.

I have found gratitude to be a vital force in my life. I've discovered that the more I focus on all the good things I have, the less I need or want, and that's a great way to live. Last year, I attended a lecture by a psychologist discussing the top benefits of a grateful mind. They were:

- The ability to reach more goals.
- Improved health.
- Better sleep and more energy.

- Increased likability amongst peers and co-workers.
- Greater support from others.
- A much healthier love life.

To reiterate, hanging a reminder note to take a deep breath throughout the day and a gratitude list on your desk can bring you many benefits and add greater value to your workday. I have found that it never hurts to be reminded continuously that some light still exists when things are at their darkest.

Most of all, never for one minute believe that your employer pays you. Your company only supplies the check; your customer fills in the blanks. Be grateful to them by demonstrating an attitude of gratitude.

Remember, you will be dealing with difficult people all of your life. It's vital to perfect your coping skills now, and then the pressure will affect you less and less. Eventually, you will be able to rise above it all, and the crazies will leave you feeling indifferent and calm.

Customer Service Soft Skill Review

Listed below are ten soft skills that you can utilize to get yourself noticed and climb the ladder at your next job. If after reading these suggestions you think they are over-simplistic-- then you're right; they are! However, how often are the basics forgotten because they are "too basic?" My prediction is that success at your next job will not be because you've got the "Midas Touch" but because you have the "People Touch."

1. Be polite, smile a lot, be kind and patient, sincerely treat your customers as if they are your best friend or relative. (Read that again, it's essential.)

2. Continuously address your customer by name. Learn to make small talk to build the relationship.

3. Become an excellent listener.

4. Relish your interactions with all of your customers-even the grumpy ones. Make them feel as if they've found a second home. Be sure they leave the interaction

feeling good about you, your company, and themselves. Please treat them with an attitude of gratitude.

5. Remember their children. Remember their names and birthdays.

6. Always ask for feedback or have a suggestion box. Remember, many fortunes were made because of the feedback customers place in a small suggestion box.

7. Accept full responsibility for errors and admit your mistakes. Always be honest. You can't always be perfect, but you must always have integrity.

8. Always deliver when promised and maybe even sooner. Instead of making outlandish promises that you can't keep, focus on being reliable.

9. Tailor to fit their needs and find unmet needs.

10. Send gifts or unique occasion cards such as anniversaries or birthdays.

11. Sincerely, say, *"Thank you for bringing this problem to my attention,"* and thanking customers for allowing you to fix their problems. Most of all, remember to say, *"Thank you for your business."*

Customer Service Interview Questions

I opened this chapter by stating that customer service and soft skills are identical twins. It doesn't matter which career you choose or the position you are applying for; you will always be involved in some type of customer service daily. I also stated that this chapter is designed to offer possible answers to probable questions you may be asked at your interview. I firmly believe that if you answer your interview questions with a "service-centered mentality," it will dramatically increase your market value. In many cases, it can help you earn a higher than expected income when it comes time for your salary negotiations.

Utilizing the information you have learned in this chapter, answer the following interview questions, and remain mindful that you may hear them again in the future.

1. We have a lot of negative customers calling during the day. Is that something you are skilled to handle, and can you give me an example?

2. Can you give me a few examples of why you think customer service is essential?

3. What soft skills do you possess that make you an effective rep, and can you give me an example?

4. How do you keep yourself calm during a difficult interaction, and can you give me an example?

5 What are some things you've done to help a customer feel comfortable and important?

6. Do you have any skills for dealing with angry customers?

Chapter 9

Soft Skills and Telephone Mastery

It happened on March 10, 1876. Alexander Graham Bell summoned his assistant, Mr. Watson, to the next room--- by telephone. That's almost 150 years ago, and since then, billions of local and long-distance telephone calls are made worldwide.

The telephone has been a fantastic tool for keeping people connected globally. In the business world, a phone is an essential tool. Professionally, you must learn to "play" your telephone as if you were playing an instrument in a finely tuned orchestra. Your telephone skills are a critical part of your business success. Your customers, clients, and managers critically judge your business savvy and judge "you as a person" according to your telephone etiquette.

6 Soft Skills Steps to Telephone Mastery

Remember, there is a chance that you'll be asked to participate in a mock phone call during your job interview. Mock or role-play calls test your phone skills, courtesies, and ability to think on your feet. Listed below are six time-tested telephone strategies. They will help you shine on the job since they are all based on professional etiquette. They will allow you to project a powerful and professional image to anyone you are dealing with over the phone. Let's go through them now:

Mastery Step 1 - Master Relaxing & Getting Focused!

The first step in telephone mastery is significant because this is where the 1st impression happens. When you pick up the phone, you must not sound rushed, confused, or unreliable. Therefore, it's essential to take a deep breath, get centered, and relax before picking up. Your customer wants to hear someone who sounds focused, intelligent, and eager to assist. If you are stressed, it changes your voice's sound and may turn off your customer. Remember to hang a small sign on your desk reminding you to take a deep breath to sound relaxed. It takes less than five seconds for your customer to formulate the 1st impression of you while on the telephone. Within those five seconds, your customer will make 1 of 5 decisions about you:

Decision 1 - They like you.

Decision 2 - They don't like you.

Decision 3 - They're indifferent about you.

Decision 4 - You sound smart.

Decision 5 - You sound like an idiot.

These decisions will then determine how the rest of the call will unfold, whether it will escalate or deescalate. Research shows that in the first five seconds:

84% of the 1st impression is based on the sound of your voice.

16% of the 1st impression is based on your words.

Therefore, at the start, your words are the least important part of the call. There is nothing more important than the sound of your voice. Make sure there isn't any food in your mouth, spit out your gum, and sound intelligently focused. Remember, the first five seconds set the stage as to how the call will unfold.

Mastery Step 2 - Master Answering Quickly!

Although it's cheaper to install an answering system in your phone services, customers still prefer speaking to a live person. I dislike pressing 1, then 2, and then pressing 3 before speaking to someone who can assist me. Regardless, industry-standard tells us to answer our business phone within the 2nd or 3rd ring or prompt. Unless your company directs you otherwise, this seems to be the professional standard. Unbelievably, answering on the very first ring may startle your client, while waiting until the 4th or 5th ring may annoy your client, especially if they are already unhappy with your services. Always remember this critical point:

"A customer will begin to mentally measure the quality of your performance before they hear your voice by the number of rings or prompts it takes to get an answer."

Mastery Step 3 - Master a Professional Greeting!

There are four steps to a professional greeting. These steps will help convince your customer that they are dealing with a professional and polished rep. Although the steps are simple, they are high on the soft skill etiquette scale. They will help you to establish instant rapport and credibility with your customers. I call them:

The 4 Answering Courtesies

Courtesy 1. Greet your customer with Good Morning, Afternoon, or Evening; NEVER, Hello!

Hello is to be utilized in your home, not your business. Some will argue that saying good morning, afternoon, or evening is inappropriate because you deal with customers in different time zones. I'm afraid I have to disagree! I find it a fantastic tool for breaking the ice and getting to know your customer a little better. If a customer contradicts your greeting by saying, *"It's not morning where they are,"* you can ask simple questions like *"May I ask, where are you calling from?"* Or *"How's the weather?"* This simple small talk can be quite useful in building rapport and a connection. Just remember not to get too personal.

Courtesy 2. Give them your company name and thank them for calling. (Say it clearly, with pride and an attitude of gratitude.)

Courtesy 3. Give them your name. (Say it clearly, and with dignity.)

Courtesy 4. Then ask, *"May I help you?"*

Research states that asking, *"Can I help you?"* may do more harm than good. While monitoring calls and consulting at a recent event, I heard a rep ask an angry customer, *"Can I help you?"* and the customer replied, *"Everyone in your company is an asshole, so I doubt you can help me!"* The more I research it, the more I believe that *"May I help you?"* is the ideal way to go. As an example, here's how we answer the phones at our company; it sounds exactly like this:

"Good Morning! Thank you for calling Jacobsen Business Seminars; this is John. May I help you?"

Mastery Step 4 - Master Crystal, Clear Diction!

Although you may have mastered the perfect greeting, your diction must also be excellent. There's nothing worse than calling a company, and you can't understand the person with whom you are speaking. Needing to ask a rep to repeat themselves is a massive inconvenience for a client, especially if you're trying to sell them something. Your customer must be able to understand every letter, syllable, and word that comes out of your mouth. It would be best if you did not speak too fast or too slow. The standard rate of speech is about 125 words per minute. It would help if you did not talk too loud or too soft. Your pitch, speed, and volume should be at a moderate level and, at the same time, sounding pleasant, friendly, and professional. Ideally, your tone and inflections should vary. These are necessary soft skills.

Since the sound of your voice plays such a significant role in excellent telephone service, you must avoid what's known as the "Top 5 Vocal Turn-Offs." My experience demonstrates that the worst reps consistently utilize these appalling vocal tones. They drastically influence your customer's attitude and rapidly create dissatisfied and angry interactions affecting your brand and apostle conversion.

The Top 5 Vocal Turn-Offs

1. **Irritated** - If a calling customer is already furious, your "irritated" sound will quickly cause an escalation. Remember, angry customers are usually looking for a fight, so don't throw out the bait or tantalize them by sounding irritated.

2. **Rushed** - Sounding rushed will cause the same reaction and outcome.

3. **Whiny** - Whining is such a horrid, high-pitched, nasal shrill that most customers will ask to speak to another rep. That kind of voice can cut through steel.

4. **Phony** - A phony sounding voice is prevalent in businesses where the reps must read scripts. Unless you're a trained actor, it's challenging for most reps to read a script and sound natural or non-mechanical. You want to avoid the humiliation of sounding like a poorly rehearsed human automaton. Remember, if you sound like a robot, they will treat you like a machine. If you work in a call center where scripts are not utilized, sounding phony should not concern you.

5. **Hesitant** - Finally, a hesitant sound quickly projects the idea that you lack confidence and don't know your job. Did you ever stop and ask someone for driving directions, and they hesitated? That usually scares me, and I end up asking someone else who can respond quickly. The quicker response makes me feel confident about you, and it sounds like you can get me to where I'm going. The hesitant response sounds like I'll end up lost.

The Top 5 Vocal Priorities

I expect that you're now ready to hear the opposite side of the coin. First, I offered you the negative vocal turn-offs; now, I'd like to share the positive vocal turn-ons. These are the essential vocal sounds you need when dealing with customers. The most successful reps earning the highest salaries consistently utilize these vocal priorities. They also achieved the most promotions. Model them, study them, practice them, and you will experience the same success. They are:

1. **Crystal, Clear Diction** - Customers cannot understand you unless you have "clear diction." In New York and New Jersey, our diction is awful, so we need to practice. Clear enunciation will place you in the top 10% of successful reps. When you answer your phone, clearly speak your professional greeting. When you say your name in the conversation, say it with a clear sound, indicating you're important and worth listening to. You must sound as if your company is worth what they are charging for their product. If you ever call a very high-end hotel, the voice that answers the phone will sound like their rooms are worth the $1000 nightly rate they are charging. On the other hand, if you call a much lower-end motel, the voice will sound like you're about to get an outstanding deal (and bed bugs). Remember, speak clearly; there is nothing worse than mumbling.

2. **Middle Range Pitch** - A middle-range pitch is also worthy to note. The middle-range will prevent you from sounding whiny or too low like a bass guitar. A high pitched voice can sound anxious at times, while a low pitched voice can sound commanding.

3. **Proper Volume** - The most important tip I can give you about volume is to project your voice, but don't shout it. If you're too loud, it can make you sound aggressive and authoritative. If you're too quiet, your customers will have trouble

hearing you. However, in many cases, a softly spoken voice can get people to listen.

4. **High Energy** – Uplifting, positive energy is happily contagious. It demonstrates your passion for the job. It also indicates your gratitude towards the customer for paying your bills and feeding your family.

5. **Enthusiasm** - Your customer must hear your enthusiasm before they can become enthusiastic about doing business with you. These are vital soft skills, tools for apostle conversion, and your ultimate success in the work-force.

Mastery Step 5 - Master Courtesy!

Use your voice to create a courteous attitude. Use your voice to indicate your willingness and enthusiasm to help. Remember, a tired voice lacking enthusiasm is very unappealing. Your voice must make the customer feel welcome. Put a smile in your voice by actually "smiling" as you are speaking with your customer. Believe me; they will sense your friendliness through the line. It may help you to tape the word "SMILE" on your receiver because your customer can hear your face. Your telephone voice must make your customer feel important, welcome, and comfortable.

Mastery Step 6 – Master Matching!

Matching the voice of the person you speak with on the phone is almost as old as the telephone itself. "Matching" is a master key for developing rapport, which eventually leads to strong connections and loyal relationships. Therefore, if your customer speaks at a fast pace, match that pace. There's nothing worse than speaking slowly while the person on the other end frantically wants to finish the call and hang up. On the other hand, if the customer speaks slower, then slow down to match it. Obviously, if they are screaming or cursing, you would **NOT** match that.

Matching is a fantastic tool that can assist you in de-escalating irate callers. Simply put, at a deep subconscious level, people like and trust people who are like them. Therefore, match their voice speed, pace, and rhythm, so you sound like them.

Most people do not want to fight or argue with themselves. Remember, the sound of your voice on the phone counts for 84%.

4 Steps for Asking to Return a Call

1. Always ask permission. (*"Mr. Rubino, with your permission, may I call you back in five minutes?"*)

2. Wait for their response.

3. Reconfirm their phone number.

4. Thank them, and return the call as promised, if not sooner.

5 Steps for Placing a Caller on Hold

1. Always ask permission. (*"Ms. Rivera, with your permission, may I place you on hold?"*)

2. Wait for their response.

3. Do not place the receiver or headset on your desk without first putting the person on hold. The caller may hear something unprofessional in the background.

4. Industry-standard and business etiquette states that you must check-up on the holding customer every two minutes.

5. When retrieving the call, **NEVER** say, *"Thank you for holding."* Instead, say, *"Thank you for your patience."*

6 Steps for Transferring a Call

1. Always ask permission. (*"Ms. Kacmarcik, with your permission, may I transfer you to Mr. Gigante?"*) Or to their voice mail.

2. Wait for their response.

3. Then, place them on hold while you check to see if Mr. Gigante is available.

4. If Mr. Gigante is open, make the transfer; if not, take a message. Be sure to give Mr. Gigante all of the caller's information and call details to be well-prepared

when he retrieves the call. The goal is that the caller does not need to rehash everything they just told you.

5. Reconfirm the caller's phone number should you get disconnected.

6. Before making the transfer, thank the customer by name.

6 Steps for Taking a Message

1. Always ask permission. (*"Ms. Rivera, with your permission, may I take a message?"*)

2. Wait for their response.

3. Since your caller has requested to speak with an unavailable party, it's essential that you collect accurate contact information from the caller. Every message you take should include:

   *The caller's first and last name name

   *The caller's business or company name

   *The best phone number to return the call

   *A summary of the purpose of the call

   *The date and time of the call

4. Review the information with the caller to confirm accuracy.

5. Assure the caller you will deliver the message and thank them for calling.

6. In **EVERY** business call scenario, **NEVER** disconnect a call until you hear the customer hang up first.

Professional Soft Skills Telephone Etiquette

I find it sad that properly executed telephone etiquette is something that is rarely noticed. However, when improperly implemented, it's glaringly apparent and calls into question your hire-ability and professionalism. Please remember:

1. Always speak directly into the mouthpiece.

2. Speak clearly! There is nothing worse than mumbling.

3. Do not eat or chew gum when you are talking on the phone.

4. Never answer on speakerphone.

5. Answer the phone with a pleasant tone regardless of whether you are busy, annoyed, or dealing with a bigger problem. The caller should not know that you are having a bad day. Remember, you need to be a good actor/actress.

6. Use a pleasant tone and do not get defensive or offensive when asked a question.

7. If someone walks into your office or over to speak to you while you are on the phone, it is vital to politely excuse yourself from the caller briefly and put him/her on hold. Apologize for the disruption and continue the phone call.

8. If you do not understand what the caller is asking or it does not make sense to you, say, *"Forgive me, could you please repeat this because I want to make sure that I understand what you are asking?"* Remain calm and collected.

9. Never tell a caller that something is not your job/dept. Because you picked up the call, it is your responsibility to get them to the right person. Let the caller know you are not equipped to help them with this particular issue, but you will find someone (or dept.) who can.

10. Phone Etiquette is required for both internal and external customers.

11. Proper telephone etiquette is something that reflects your skills.

12. Failure to practice proper phone etiquette can cost you your job.

Take Caution in what you Say:

DON'T SAY:	DO SAY:
"Who's calling?"	*"May I ask who's calling?"*
"They have not come in yet."	*"She's not in her office at the moment."*
"He's on his third coffee break."	*"He's away from his desk at the moment."*
"He left early today."	*"He's on an assignment until tomorrow."*

13 Steps for Assertively Dealing with Irates on the Phone

1. Never, Never, Ever, Ever, interrupt an irate, **EVER!** Let them spew their venom and run out of steam, first.

2. When it's your turn to speak, lower your voice.

3. Stay calm and focus only on the situation or goal.

4. Don't take it personally; instead, take it professionally. That's what you're getting paid to do.

5. Give them your full attention and **SOUND** (84%) like you **WANT TO HELP**.

6. Calmly repeat or re-state back everything you heard to be sure you clearly understand.

7. Pretend you are helping a family member or best friend.

8. Apply the professional apology, if needed.

9. Act quickly and effectively, telling them the steps you will take and how soon.

10. **ALWAYS** ask how else you can be of service. **(ESSENTIAL)**

11. **ALWAYS** thank them for doing business with you.

12. **ALWAYS** follow-up!

13. Use the **L.A.S.T** approach.

Here Are Some Soft Skill Questions:

1. Do you answer the phone with a polished, professional greeting?

2. Do you have clear, understandable diction?

3. Do you speak too quickly or mumble?

4. Do you sound human or like a robot?

5. Do you commit any of the five vocal turn-offs?

6. Are you polished in regards to the five vocal priorities?

7. Do you agree that these vocal tools and courtesies can build relationships?

8. What is the most important rule for placing a caller on hold?

9. What is the most important rule for transferring a caller?

10. What is the most important rule when asking to return a call?

Chapter 9 Review

1. Master relaxing & getting focused. Take a deep breath before picking up the call.

2. Master answering quickly.

3. Master a professional greeting.

4. Say your name with clear diction, pride, and enthusiasm.

5. Master crystal, clear diction.

6. Master courtesy.

7. Match their voice speed, pace & rhythm.

8. If you sound like a robot, they will treat you like a machine.

9. You must always sound sincere, not rehearsed.

10. Avoid *"Can I help you?"* Stick with *"May I help you?"*

Telephone Interview questions

Utilizing the information you have learned in this chapter, answer the following interview questions, and remain mindful that you may hear them again in the future.

1. At our company, it's essential to make positive connections with our customers as soon as you pick up the phone. Can you give me a few examples of how you have done this in the past?

2. Can you tell me how you de-escalate an angry caller and give me an example?

3. Tell me why you are the perfect candidate to handle demanding customers?

4. Are you open to role-playing a "mock call" with me now?

5. What do you do to sound enthusiastic on the phone?

6. How do you prevent angry customers from draining your energy?

Chapter 10

Soft Skills and Dealing with Conflict

This chapter contains many practical problem-solving, conflict resolution tools I'm sure you'll appreciate, especially if you're applying for a supervisory or leadership position. If you are a master at resolving conflict, your employability factor is exceptionally high. Employers are hiring candidates who can create "win-win" outcomes with the staff, team, or management. Possessing a solution-oriented mindset is an exceptional soft skill.

Conflict is inevitable because of human differences. It's something that has always been around and will never go away. That is especially true in the business world, where all of your problems come on two legs and talk back. Conflict on a team is as important as good communication skills. It creates a phenomenon known as "creative abrasion," which helps improve the way teams communicate, make decisions, and solve problems. Conflict should not be feared but embraced. It would be best if you did not ignore conflict but address it. If handled correctly and in a timely fashion, conflict can bring you many benefits, blessings, and advantages.

"The only time conflict is harmful is if it escalates."

Since the beginning of time, every significant human achievement was born out of the ashes of a conflict? It's true! Buckminster Fuller once said, *"Whatever humans have learned had to be learned as a consequence of the trial and error experience."* Conflict has been a considerable resource and ally for anyone desiring change. The words "conflict" & "change" are synonymous.

While I'm not asking you to create a conflict calculatingly, I invite you to view your conflicts in a different light. Change your perceptions about them. With the right attitude and appropriate communication skills, your conflicts will become a powerful tool for creating positive change and growth. This rule applies to your family and business life.

I want to introduce you to a progressive conflict resolution strategy that I've seen produce impressive, powerful results. I call it **"The 5 Steps to Cooperative**

Resolution." While these steps are common sense, I've noticed that common sense is not all that common in highly charged conflicts. People know the rules, yet anger and frustration can cause us to forget our manners and trigger a conflict escalation. Anger can cloud your judgment and cause your mouth to work faster than your mind.

The 5 Steps to Cooperative Resolution

Step 1 - Prevent the Conflict from Escalating.

I mentioned that all conflict in your professional and personal life could be your ally unless they escalate. You can prevent conflict escalation by confronting the problem, person, or situation immediately. **NEVER WAIT!** The moment a conflict appears---confront! My experience has consistently shown me that most conflicts escalate because someone did not nip them in the bud instantaneously. The longer you wait to confront, the more intense and problematic your conflict will grow. The longer you wait to confront, the more you're rewarding the negative behavior. In many cases, this will damage relationships.

My research indicates that the number one reason people avoid immediate confrontation is a term called "Confrontation Phobia." People are afraid of rocking the boat. People are fearful of starting trouble or hurting someone's feelings. I believe this phobia is born out of a misunderstanding of what a confrontation actually is.

Power <u>Over</u> Someone vs. Power <u>With</u> Someone

Confrontations are not about having power over someone, pushing them into a corner, and angrily telling them off. Confrontations are not about an aggressive "power over" approach. But instead an assertive "power with" mindset. The "power over" approach thinks and speaks words such as *"Let me set you straight!" "I'm going to tell you off!" "I'm gonna fix you!"*

The "power with" approach thinks and speaks words such as *"How can we work this out together?" "Let's sit down and discuss how we can both benefit from these circumstances."* It's a kinder, gentler approach that will lower their defenses and drop their guard because they won't feel as if you're attacking them. It's less stressful and much easier to confront someone assertively. Confrontation phobia disappears when you offer to help rather than criticize, find fault, or condemn.

Exceptions to the Rule

I know you've heard the expression *"there are exceptions to the rule."* The same is true with confrontation. Although immediate confrontation is the safest, fastest method to prevent conflict escalation, there are two exceptions to the rule.

> A. **NEVER** confront anyone in public. If your goal is to be a team leader, I'm sure you don't want to humiliate or embarrass your people. Therefore, all confrontations must be conducted privately. On a personal note, if you do confront, mock, humiliate, embarrass, ridicule, or criticize your team publically, you're not a leader; you're a loser.
>
> B. **NEVER** confront if you need to cool your head or calm yourself down. Remember, if you bring anger to a confrontation, it will backfire on you. Wait an hour until you calm down. Go for a walk, wash your face, or get a drink. But only confront when you're relaxed and focused. Soft skills at their finest!

Step 2 - Set an appointment for problem-solving.

> A. The sooner, the better.

Step 3 - Together, brainstorm solutions for *BOTH* parties.

I recommend approaching the brainstorming process with care. Remember, your goal is not only to resolve the issue but to preserve the relationship. Here, your soft skills are essential.

It's ideal to meet in a place away from where the problem originated. Negative emotions from the surrounding environment may cause the person to put up their guard, making troubleshooting more difficult. A favorite tactic is to conduct your problem-solving session outside of the office or in a restaurant while having breakfast, lunch, or dinner.

The most positive approach to begin a resolution process is to meet and greet the other party with an optimistic statement. It sets the stage for a friendly discussion and increases your chance of a win-win by 47%. Several good opening remarks may be:

"I'm glad we can get together and resolve this issue."

"I'm sure we can agree swiftly."

"Thank you for your determination in bringing this issue to an end."

Make sure you use "I" statements and speak in an even, conversational tone. That will help to build trust and create a lot of rapport, essential for problem-solving. Also, avoid bringing up the past and instead focus only on the topic at hand. These ideas will also help the other party feel more comfortable and maintain their composure.

Most of all, continually focus on areas that you have in common. Finding common ground in a resolution process allows you to see solutions you may have overlooked.

During the session, I recommend that you and the other party sit facing each other without a desk or table between you. Sitting behind a desk acts as a "divider" and sends a subconscious signal to the other party that you're on "opposite sides." That signal will cause them to feel threatened and raise their guard. The most successful and rapid problem-solving sessions are conducted without desks.

You can also increase your brainstorming session's effectiveness by using their name often without overdoing it. Always discuss problems before solutions, and start with the easy issues before moving to the more difficult ones. Solving easy problems first builds confidence and creates momentum with the other party.

As a unique problem-solving note: Never ask people to "feel differently," or "be different," or to "change their attitude." These are requests that you do not have the right to ask of any human being. Remember, in conflict resolution; you are only permitted to request "behavioral changes." The actual magic of conflict lies not in trying to change others but to use conflict as a stepping stone toward greater working relationships and more effective resolution skills.

Step 4 - Get the agreement in writing.

When you arrive at an agreeable solution, you must then get the agreement in writing. You may spend hours, days, or weeks in the resolution process. Yet if the completed deal is not in writing, you wasted all of your time and energy. Remember, if it's not in writing, it never happened. Although a written agreement may not be appropriate in the family arena, it's still essential for everyone to agree to the new terms.

Step 5 - Set a follow-up date. (If necessary)

7 Part Confrontation Script

Below is an "assertive, power with" script I've been successfully using for decades. It consists of seven parts designed to create a relaxed, peaceful confrontation without building fear, resentment, or hard feelings. For you to be successful utilizing this script, it's ideal that you commit it to memory. Each part has a psychological impact helping to create cooperative resolution.

Part 1 – Confront with a win-win attitude.

The research concludes that your attitude significantly impacts how the confrontation will unfold in the first five minutes. Therefore, approach the person, persons, or team with a win-win mindset. Remember, the first five minutes set the stage for your failure or success.

"Excuse me, Joe, do you have a minute? I need to speak with you?"

    A. Always use their name.

    B. Give them the "Yes Visual" when you ask if they have a minute.

Part 2 – Introduce the conversation.

"I've noticed that............................"

    A. Use an even, conversational tone and explain the details of the issue.

    B. Sound concerned.

Part 3 – State the impact of the behavior.

"When our customers come in here, I want them to know you're the professional I know you are."

    A. Use an even, conversational tone.

    B. Sound concerned.

    C. Act like you want to help.

Part 4 – Ask them for feedback.

"What are your thoughts?"

This part is what makes a good leader and coach. It's easier to solve a problem if you allow the person to develop their own solution rather than offering your advice. Research suggests that when people develop their own solutions, they are more likely to follow through and succeed.

    A. Use an even, conversational tone.

    B. Sound concerned.

    C. Act like you want to help.

Part 5 – Ask permission to guide them.

If they don't offer any solutions when you ask for their thoughts, you will need to jump in with your own.

"With your permission, may I make a suggestion?"

    A. When you ask this question, give them the "Yes Visual."

    B. Wait for a response before you offer a suggestion.

Part 6 – Politely close the deal.

"Would you be willing to do that?"

    A. When you ask this question, give them the "Yes Visual."

Part 7 – Always thank them!

Thanking is an essential soft skill we've discussed many times in this book.

Conflict is Inevitable because of Human Differences

I'd like to take a moment now and explain the various outcomes you can expect during a resolution process. Depending on your problem-solving abilities or skills, experts in the field tell us you can expect 1 of 5 outcomes during a problem-solving process. I'd like to offer you a "possible 6th outcome" that most people never discuss or teach. However, I believe it's the most important and valuable of all.

There Are 3 Types of Conflicts:

1. **Unilateral** - Over 65% of all conflicts are *unilateral or personal problems,* meaning you can resolve them independently without involving any outside help.

2. **Bi-lateral** - A *bilateral* conflict involves two people or parties, and both are required for the resolution to transpire.

3. **Joint** - The third is a *joint* conflict, typically involving small or large groups of people or teams. In many cases, joint conflicts require 3rd party resolution experts, facilitators, and mediators.

With the right tools and common sense, 80% of conflicts can be resolved. Unfortunately, with the right tools and common sense, some conflicts cannot be resolved. That is because some people thrive on creating conflict and spreading negativity. Some people don't get ulcers; they're just carriers.

There Are 2 Reasons for Bilateral or Joint Conflicts:

1. We Have *Different* Interests.

For example:

    A. I want to go out to dinner, and you want to stay home.
    B. I want to move to Florida, and you prefer California.
    C. I want to be on your team, and you are not interested in working with me.
    D. I want to resolve an issue, and you can't be bothered. You don't care.

2. We Have the *Same* Interests, Which Are in Conflict.

For example:

- A. We're both applying for the same job position.
- B. Some new office space just became available, and we both want it.
- C. We both want the same week off for vacation, and it's not realistic for the company.
- D. I want to sell my car, and you want to buy it. My asking price is $10,000, and you only want to pay $7500.

When resolving conflict with the tools and strategies discussed earlier, the problem can usually have any 1 of 5 outcomes:

1. Win-Lose.

In this scenario, I win, and you lose. This outcome is beneficial for me and unfortunate for you. I walk away from the negotiation table smiling, and you walk away, harboring bitterness and resentment. This result leaves the problem unresolved in your mind, and chances are incredibly high that I have not heard the last of you. This issue will quickly rise again, and we'll both be back at the negotiation table soon.

2. Lose-Win.

In this scenario, I lose, and you win. This outcome is beneficial for you and unfortunate for me. You walk away from the negotiation table smiling, and I walk away, harboring bitterness and resentment. This result leaves the problem unresolved in my mind, and chances are incredibly high that you have not heard the last of me. This issue will quickly rise again, and we'll both be back at the negotiation table soon.

3. Lose-Lose.

Here is a familiar scenario, especially for those with weak communication, problem-solving, and negotiation skills. It's also widespread for people who lose their tempers quickly or don't know what they want. Interestingly, for negative people, this outcome is considered an opportunity for revenge. Their warped thought process is that *"I may have lost, but at least I took you with me."*

4. Compromise.

To compromise is to make a deal between different parties where each party gives up part of their demand. In this outcome, all parties win and lose simultaneously. In other words, they each get a little of what they want--- and don't want. A compromise is a standard resolution tactic found in politics.

5. Win-Win.

Win-Win is a term made famous by Steven Covey in his fantastic book, "The 7 Habits of Highly Effective People." Win-Win is sometimes misunderstood and must be clarified because a win-win can take on <u>two</u> acceptable forms.

A. Win-Win means everyone concerned has all of their demands or requests met to the fullest extent. In other words, everyone gets what they want, and they live happily ever after. This outcome is possible and happens sometimes.

B. Win-Win does not necessarily mean you'll get everything you want or all of your demands met. It does mean that all parties concerned get so much of what they wanted, including some unexpected extra bonuses, that everyone walks away from the table satisfied with no underlying bitterness.

Therein lies a critical distinction, so let's review it.

"A Win-Win does not necessarily mean you will have all of your demands met. However, all parties concerned get so much of what they wanted, including extra unexpected perks and benefits, that everyone walks away from the table satisfied with no underlying bitterness."

If there is ever any underlying bitterness, resentment, or hostility, it is **not** considered a Win-Win. Instead, it is a compromise.

Creating a Win-Win outcome during a resolution process requires a unique set of common denominators. These five denominators must be brought to the decision table before problem-solving begins:

A. Both parties are very sincere and committed to resolving the issue.

B. Both parties have a strong desire for mutual gain. (Assertive. Let's both win!)

C. Both parties are excellent communicators.

D. Both parties know exactly what they want.

E. Both parties have good negotiation skills.

I mentioned earlier, there is a 6th outcome that I enjoy sharing in my seminars. All of my participants appreciate the insight, and it's always very well received. It's an outcome not readily discussed in conflict resolution strategies, but I find it an enlightened route for those seeking real value in their problem-solving abilities. I call it:

6. Win-Win-Heal!

Win-Win-Heal is very similar to a Win-Win. A Win-Win-Heal will have the identical outcomes as a standard Win-Win. The massive distinction lies in the fact that both parties' relationship is wholly healed, repaired, and in a better place **AFTER** the Win-Win is achieved. This mindset is an enlightened way to resolve problems because its focus is on **mutual gain** and **relationship enrichment**. This worldview completely surpasses the people who only rush to the table to see what they can get without regard for the other parties' interests.

Perhaps one day, our political, national, and global measuring stick for determining your problem-solving skills will not only be judged by how many resolutions you've achieved but also by how many relationships you've restored along the way.

When's the Best Time to Avoid Conflict?

The fastest way to reduce any apprehension towards conflict is to accept it as an inescapable part of our life and world. An important fact worth repeating is that conflict is inevitable because of human differences.

Research from the Virginia Department of Human Resource Management states that "60 to 80 percent of all workplace conflict stems from strained or tense relationships between employees and executives." More proof that conflict is usually not far behind when people are involved.

Although most of us would rather avoid or circumvent conflict any time it occurs, I mentioned, it may not always be a good idea because of the significant positive benefits an adequately resolved conflict can create. If you practice and apply the communication tools, soft skills, and problem-solving strategies we've discussed, conflict can bring you blessings.

Adequately resolved conflict creates a unity of purpose, heals relationships, improves communication, and more importantly, leads directly to successful future collaborations. Indeed, if the dispute is handled correctly, it can also lead to better decision-making and enhanced creativity.

Regardless, for many people avoiding conflict is often the easiest way to deal with it. However, "avoiding" does not make the conflict disappear. Instead, it pushes it under the surface for a while until it reappears in a more monstrous form.

Irrespective of the benefits conflict resolution can bring, research concludes that there are four specific conflict situations worth avoiding if it is within your power to do so. Regardless of your conflict resolution skill level, becoming entangled with these four types of conflict will usually create a "lose-lose" outcome.

1. Avoid Conflicts About Rules & Regulations.

At this point, most people would ask, *"If I avoid conflicts revolving around rules and regulations, how can I change outdated policies, procedures, and processes?"* That's a great question! While I believe that a single person acting alone can change the world, statistically speaking, this type of conflict is easier to resolve if it involves a group effort rather than one sole person. If you alone possess the proper communication tools, people skills, and problem-solving strategies—go for it! If not, this is an excellent conflict to avoid unless you have a strong team behind you.

2. Avoid Conflicts Threatening Your Job or Security.

I would think that this one was a no-brainer, but apparently, it is not. If someone puts a gun to your head and demands your money, it's not the time to whip out your conflict resolution guidebook to decide your next move. It's also not the right opportunity to try out your bargaining and negotiation skills. One of my favorite expressions is to *"Choose your battles wisely."* This particular conflict situation may be a perfect time to keep that expression in mind and intelligently weigh your pros and cons before tackling this kind of conflict.

3. Avoid Conflicts Challenging Core Beliefs or Values.

Unless your favorite pastime is sharpening your argumentative skills, this is a significant conflict to avoid. Conflicts concerning religion or politics are on the top of this list. People's psychological makeup is a construction of their beliefs and values. Their ideas and values create who they are. By asking people to alter their values, you're asking them to modify their individuality and internal wiring completely. This is a good conflict to avoid because it's difficult getting people to see out of their self-constructed box. Also, these conflicts tend to escalate quickly. However, if you have time to waste and enjoy arguing—go for it!

4. Avoid Conflicts Where the Other Party Does Not Want to Resolve.

This situation is the most difficult of all to cope with and the most difficult to accept. It can be challenging if it encompasses a family relationship. However, the fact is that some people do not want to resolve or "play nice." Some people need time to cool down, and some people get stuck in their viewpoint and can't think or see out of that box. This is a good conflict to avoid because you may be spinning your wheels and wasting valuable time on a person or issue that may not be worth it. As a last resort, this is the perfect conflict situation where a mediator may prove to be particularly valuable.

When to Walk Away from a Conflict…and not Look Back!

A Parable

A monkey shoved his hand and arm into a long-necked bottle to grab some peanuts that were lying on the bottom. When his hand was full, he ran into a small dilemma. His tightly closed fist packed with peanuts was now too large to retrieve from the bottle's thin neck. His hand and arm fit neatly in and out of the bottle while his hand was empty, but the moment he made a fist - he was stuck.

The moral of this parable is that sometimes we have to learn to "let go."

What happens when you've applied every strategy, technique, and resolution tactic and nothing helps? What happens when you invest hours or years in a resolution process only to end up in a position that's worse than where you started? When is the best time to just walk away, let go and not look back?

That is an awkward position because walking away is the absolute last resort when everything else has failed. You may have to permanently say goodbye to a career, a job, or a relationship. Here is a critical point to remember:

"When you decide to walk, your timing must be perfect, or you may suffer some personal or professional setbacks."

For example, some people walk away **"too early"** and regret not giving it one more chance or trying a different resolution approach. Walking away too early can also deprive you of the resolution skills and lessons you could have developed by sticking around or working harder. Remember, every conflict you resolve helps to perfect your resolution skills.

Some people in battered relationships wait around and leave **"too late."** In many cases, they end up emotionally and physically maltreated and scarred. On the other hand, some people **"never walk away"** and live a life of inner and outer turmoil with a complete sense of hopelessness.

Walking away may be the best option after you have used all your power to resolve a conflict without positive results.

Research into human problem solving concludes that if you can answer "Yes" to any one of the following three questions, you are in a perfect position to let go and walk away. Your timing will be in alignment with your values. Therefore, any regrets or guilt can be minimized. If you answer "Yes" to all three--- perhaps you should have already walked a long time ago.

Question # 1 - Am I putting in more than I'm getting out?

That is an excellent and insightful question simply because if you're exerting tremendous energy without reaping any benefits, the chances are that same pattern will continue long into your future. If you find yourself answering "Yes" to this question, you must ask yourself, *"Is this a price I'm willing to pay?"* In this particular situation, your "cost" may far outweigh the "price."

Question # 2 - Is the conflict damaging the relationship?

Walking away and letting go may prove an excellent solution if the conflict is causing relationship damage. In this case, the question to ask yourself is, *"Am I willing to lose or permanently damage this relationship so I can win?"* Another issue is, *"Can I live happily in this situation if the conflict is left unresolved?"* If your answer is "Yes," focus on the more positive aspects of the relationship and drop the conflict.

Question # 3 - Is the conflict damaging me?

That is the most critical question of all. How is this conflict destroying you personally? Is your health at stake? Is your sanity impaired? Is your safety threatened in any way? Will remaining in this career, job, or relationship create irreparable damage in your life? If the answer is "Yes," let go and walk away and quickly.

The 3 Shifts

Walking away requires what I call **"The 3 Shifts."** You must shift your mind, your heart, and your body.

1. You **shift your mind** and perceptions to a place that realizes you've done everything in your power to no avail.

2. You **shift your heart** by sincerely forgiving yourself and the party involved.

3. Finally, **you shift your body** by turning it towards the door, confidently moving your legs in a forward motion, and preventing your head from ever turning back.

I want to close with a thought-provoking parable that neatly sums up the information just discussed. It's called...

"The Bear that wouldn't Stop Crying."

While walking in a zoo, a man noticed a large bear hysterically crying, sobbing, and moaning. *"Why is that large brown bear crying,"* the man curiously asked the zookeeper? *"Because that bear is sitting on a large rusty nail,"* responded the zookeeper. More puzzled, the man asked, *"Why doesn't the bear get off the nail if it hurts so much?"* The zookeeper looked at the man and said, *"The nail hurts just enough to make him cry, but <u>not</u> enough to make him move."*

The moral is do not wait until things are so bad or hurt so much that you are forced to change. Make the necessary changes now. Don't wait until it hurts enough.

Chapter 10 Review

1. Hiring managers are looking for candidates who can resolve and communicate through conflict.

2. If you apply for a managerial, supervisory, or leadership position, conflict resolution skills are imperative.

3. The most successful team leaders view conflict as a tool that can improve a team's effectiveness and productivity.

4. The ideal situation is to prevent the conflict from escalating.

5. Set up a neutral location for the resolution session.

6. Brainstorm various solutions and remain open to all possibilities.

7. Put the agreement in writing.

8. Only request behavioral changes.

9. Avoid conflicts regarding rules & regulations.

10. Avoid conflicts where your security or job is threatened.

11. Avoid conflicts where core beliefs or values are challenged.

12. Avoid conflicts where the other party has no interest in resolving.

Possible Interview Questions

Utilizing the information you have learned in this chapter, answer the following interview questions, and remain mindful that you may hear them again in the future.

1. Tell me about a time you resolved a conflict with your team and the steps you applied to accomplish the resolution?

2. Give me an example of how you would guide your team through a difficult conflict?

3. What are some of your favorite problem-solving communication tools, and give me an example of how they've helped you?

Chapter 11

Mastering Your Time and Enhancing Your Productivity

Technically, time management is not a soft skill. However, I'm including this information because managing your time is an imperative "work readiness" skill. It can help you get noticed by superiors while quickly climbing the ladder of success at work or home. Attendees in my classes report that at 45% of their interviews, the hiring manager asked how they managed their time. Therefore, including some tips and skills in this book will only serve to benefit you.

There are thousands of great books and videos available to you regarding this topic. I've read, studied, taught, and applied almost all of them. Over the decades, I've stockpiled, correlated, and prioritized this information, breaking it down to what I believe are the most important concepts for you to learn and master.

Time is an Illusion Created by the Human Mind

I'll begin with the **SINGLE MOST IMPORTANT** concept you can learn about mastering your time, and that is "time is an illusion created by your mind." Time is a figment of your imagination or a mental deception. Time is not real.

"If time were "real," it wouldn't drag for some and fly for others at the same event."

How is it possible that a two-hour event can feel as if it lasted ten hours to one person and only a few minutes to another person? Why does time fly for some and linger for others? The answer is because our internal perception of events creates time, not our clocks, calendars, or day planners. "Real-Time" happens in our mind. Perhaps this is why so many of us own the most expensive cell phones containing the best time management apps, the most sophisticated clocks and calendars, top of the line day planners, and we still can't get our friggin lives together. Why? Because you can't manage time by relying on external devices when "real-time" is created inside of you.

We know for a fact that your attitude the first five minutes of the day sets the stage and dictates how your day will unfold. If your first thoughts in the morning are, *"Today is going to suck!"* Chances are your day will drag and suck. And your clock and day planner bear no responsibility for it. If your first thoughts in the morning are, *"This is going to be a great day, and I can handle anything that comes my way."* The chances are good; that will be your outcome.

Now, let me be very clear. I'm not knocking watches, clocks, or day planners. I successfully use them daily. I am saying they are to be used only as tools to keep us focused, minimize distractions, and show us if we are hitting our mark.

"So, the first rule in time mastery is for you to get your head straight."

The first five minutes before you begin your day, or sit down to start a big project, tackle a new task, or rewrite your resume, "think" that it will be "easy." **Think** that the answers and creative ideas will flow to you. **Think** that you will complete this task successfully and on time. I promise you will be more productive than if you began with a dark, pessimistic attitude. Perhaps you'll discover that you were not as busy as you initially thought. Maybe you are simply standing in your own way. Remember, your attitude; the first five minutes are your golden opportunity to "save time" by getting things done right the first time.

Are You An ETM?

"Effective Time Managers" (ETMs) earned that title because they effectively manage time. When you study and observe ETMs, you will notice they have three distinct traits in common:

1. They finish all their projects on time or early.
2. Their work is always accurate.
3. They are rarely stressed while working.

At your next job, I want you to walk in the door your first day as an accomplished ETM. It's the perfect way to begin a new career and get yourself noticed. For newly hired employees, I call this the "Halo-Effect." The art of immediately getting positively and enthusiastically noticed by your managers or supervisors and branded a "superstar" employee.

The 7 Time Wasters and Productivity Zappers

ETMs do a lot of things right, and there are certain activities they avoid entirely. Research indicates that the seven activities listed below waste precious time and cause productivity to falter. You must avoid them or learn to work around them professionally and personally. If you have trouble in any of these areas, work on one "time zapper" at a time until you perfect it. Then, move to the next. It's the fastest way to conquer them all.

1. Multi-tasking – Multi-tasking has a nickname, "The Big Lie." Unbelievably, multi-tasking is not a useful tool for effectively managing time. There are thousands of documented medical and psychological studies stating that the human brain can only think one thought at a time. There are also thousands of documented medical and psychological studies proving that it's more effective to do one task at a time than to multi-task.

Multi-tasking is good for "low-brain" activities such as watching TV and eating at the same time. "High brain" activities such as large or technical tasks or texting while driving is complicated for the brain to accomplish. This is why so many people are hurt or killed each year trying to text and drive. The brain is simply not hard-wired for high-brain multi-tasking skills. ETMs concentrate on one thing at a time and don't stop or move on until the task is completed.

2. Failing to manage distractions - I recently took a three-hour flight from Texas to Philly. I accomplished more in that three-hour flight than I usually complete in a full day. The secret – there were no distractions! Daily, we are interrupted every three minutes on average. It then takes the brain about twenty-three minutes to reboot, get back on track, and focused. Even more disconcerting is that we are still being interrupted every three minutes within the twenty-three minutes that the brain tries to refocus.

Considering we discussed the mind earlier and its role in time management, here is what's interesting. The research concludes that 80% of your daily distractions are mental distractions, such as your mind wandering, daydreaming, or worrying. The other 20% of daily distractions are tangible or physical, such as your phone ringing, someone knocking on your door, loud, chatty co-workers, or receiving an email or text. Isn't that interesting? That means 80% of your daily distractions are self-created and self-inflicted. That's great news! Once you realize you're doing it all to yourself, then you acquire the power to stop doing it to yourself. Instead of worrying and dreading the emails, calls, unexpected visitors, and loud co-workers, change your perception about them. Your new, empowering perception will quickly reduce your stress and anxiety levels; you'll be more in control, more empowered, and more productive. Why? Because it's easier to control what's happening in your mind than to control people or events.

3. Procrastination – ETMs never procrastinate! There are many ways to avoid success, but procrastination is one of the fastest ways to fail in every area of your life. Procrastinators sabotage themselves on purpose by placing mental obstacles in their own path, harming their performance. Research indicates that 20% of people identify themselves as chronic procrastinators. For them, procrastination is a lifestyle, although a maladaptive one. Procrastinators use their minds differently than non-procrastinators. Also, non-procrastinators use their minds differently than procrastinators. Once again, procrastination is a mental or psychological thing.

For example, if you notice that your kitchen sink is stacked with dirty dishes, and you begin to imagine the effort and time it will take to clean each plate by hand, one by one. Chances are incredibly high that you will be de-motivated and quickly procrastinate. On the other hand, if you imagine the sink empty and clean, that mental image will motivate you to act and get busy. Therefore, the leading cause of procrastination is where you have your focus. If you focus on the task, all the complex steps in between, and the hard work required, you will procrastinate. Focusing and dwelling on the process is a demotivator.

"Complexity is the enemy of execution."

ETMs focus only on the outcome. The steps in between or process are essential and must be tackled, but if you keep your mind focused on the goal, your motivation to act increases significantly. If you keep your focus on your end-result or completed outcome, that positive, less stressful image will motivate you into action. Procrastinators don't need schedules, calendars, lists, or time management skills. Procrastinators need to form a new habit of focusing on the "end result" or "outcome" of their projects or tasks. The way you think determines whether you will follow through, and better thinking always creates better results.

"Remember, the #1 cause of procrastination is focusing on the task rather than the outcome."

4. Taking on too much or more than you can handle – This time zapper is very common in the business world. Sometimes employees want to impress a superior, and others just can't say "no." The first step here is to **make peace** with the fact that you cannot get everything done simultaneously. Unless you wear a red cape and large **S** on your chest, you'll need to come up with a better plan.

ETMs begin first with the task that is the most time-sensitive. Ask your manager which task is a top priority? Then, focus on completing that task with positive intention and enthusiasm. It's extremely healthy if you do your work with a happy heart. In many cases, it's helpful to defer, delegate, and eliminate by asking for help.

5. Not taking breaks – Would you like to improve your daily productivity dramatically? Try taking a break. Statistically, people who do not take their breaks or skip lunch have a drastic 61% drop in productivity. In many industries, lunch breaks are getting shorter or even nonexistent. According to a survey by a workplace consulting group "Right Management," only one in five office workers report taking an actual lunch break away from their desk, Yet taking a break, even for fifteen to twenty minutes—is a proven way to support your concentration and energy levels throughout the day. All the tasks and decisions we make daily gradually depletes our psychological resources. Employees who take breaks always outperform those who do not.

Recently, a gentleman in one of my classes asked, *"I work an eight hour day, I have fifteen minutes for lunch, and breaks in between are not permitted; what should I do?"* I told him, **"QUIT!"**

6. Ineffectively scheduling tasks – ETMs make lists. They follow their list seamlessly. Lists help keep you on track, prevent distractions, prevent repetitive labor, and a list never forgets.

Many great apps are available to help you schedule and maintain a list, but I'm more effective at writing my list on paper the old-fashioned way. Here are a few tips to make your list functional.

A. If you write your list the night before, you will see a 25% increase in your productivity the next day.

B. Write your list at the same time every day, preferably five minutes before you leave the office.

C. Never prioritize your schedule; instead, schedule your priorities.

D. Keep your list where you can see it.

E. As you complete tasks, cross them off and add items as they arise.

F. Crossing items off your list creates excitement, motivation, and momentum.

G. Every minute you spend planning saves five to ten minutes in execution.

7. A messy desk – Are you "debris dysfunctional," "organizationally challenged," or suffer from "possession obsession?" If so, you're in a club in which many Americans belong. My wife has one of the sloppiest desks I've ever seen. She calls it an "organized mess." Amazingly, while blind-folded, she can find anything on that desk, including alphabetized files. While some people will argue that a messy desk is a perfect way to work, statistically, a messy desk causes a 32% drop in productivity. However, if you find it impossible to work unless your desk is cluttered, it's beneficial to clean your desk before leaving your shift. Research indicates that starting your day with a clean, fresh, organized desk sets the stage for a productive day.

Chapter 11 Review

1. Get your mind and attitude straight before anything else.

2. Take caution in what you focus on.

3. Finish a task before moving on to the next.

4. Begin making a list and reviewing it the night before.

Test Your Time Management Skills with this Quiz

1. Do you plan tomorrow's work today? **Yes/ No**
2. Do you perform important tasks at your daily "high energy" peak? **Yes/ No**
3. Do you get unpleasant duties out of the way as soon as possible? **Yes/ No**
4. Do you "visualize" a successful day before leaving your home? **Yes/ No**
5. Are you able to deal bluntly with people who waste your time? **Yes/ No**
6. Do you "log" how long it takes to accomplish each day's tasks? **Yes/ No**
7. Do you get things done as promised on time? **Yes/ No**
8. Do you set aside a portion of each day to think, create, and plan? **Yes/ No**
9. Is your desk or workplace tidy? Can you find what you need? **Yes/ No**
10. Do you use a "list" to manage and complete your tasks? **Yes/ No**
11. Do you know how to choose your most productive tasks? **Yes/ No**
12. Do you know exactly what your top priorities are? **Yes/ No**

Evaluating your score:

- If you responded **"yes" to 10-12** of the questions above, you excellently handle your time.

- If you responded **"yes" to 7-9** of the questions, you are good but still have room to grow.

- If you responded **"yes" to 6 or below,** you are wasting valuable time and may not even know it.

Chapter 12

HOT Networking Tips!

Networking is a beneficial tool for landing an interview. Whether you're networking on social media platforms such as LinkedIn or live (in-person) interactions, you must master this critical art to survive and surpass your competition. This chapter will focus on networking strategies at live gatherings since soft skills are more prevalent.

The most popular live networking events are small or large meetings, job fairs, social events, conferences, luncheons, trade shows, fundraisers, sporting events, or your local commerce chamber. The primary goal of networking is to meet people who will help you land an interview and a job. I've been networking throughout my entire business career. I find it a lot of fun meeting new people, finding common ground, and trying to make a connection. However, I've also had times when my networking experiences were tiresome and hectic. I value my time and do not want to waste it by attending networking events and coming up empty-handed.

The following **HOT** networking tips are for you. After years of networking trial and error, I've utilized the following strategies to make good first impressions, meet the right people, and follow-thru with follow-up. It's critical for you to "shine" at networking events because you only have fifteen seconds to impress a possible hiring manager, so you want to do it right the first time--- every time. I know these tips will help you to perfect your networking talents. Naturally, the more events you attend, the faster you'll polish your skills and increase your chances of being hired.

1. **Arrival Time:** I always like to arrive at an event 10 minutes early. That gives me time to meet the people in charge, and they usually introduce me to other important people before the event begins. It also allows me the opportunity to check out the room and start remembering names. However, the same applies to an actual job interview. You do not want to arrive too early, and you never want to arrive late. Soft Skills and business etiquette indicate that 10 minutes early is the sweet spot.

2. **Your Attire:** How you dress is critical; it helps create an excellent first impression. Clean, casual business attire is expected. No distasteful or revealing clothing EVER! Be sure all your zippers are zipped, shoes polished, teeth cleaned, fresh breath, neat hair, and clean nails. Once again, it takes just fifteen seconds to create a first impression. (Don't take this lightly!)

3. **Cell Phones:** You must turn your cell phone OFF at a job fair or interview. I've seen more people lose out on great employment opportunities because their phone rang or vibrated at the wrong time than I care to recall.

4. **Your Entrance:** As you enter an event, take caution in speaking to and dealing with the receptionist. The receptionist is the hiring manager's gatekeeper and reports any rude, arrogant, or obnoxious people directly to the hiring manager. One of the fastest ways to lose an employment opportunity is to disrespect the receptionist. In 90% of the companies I've done training for, the hiring manager asked the receptionist about their first impressions of the candidate. And over 90% of the time, the hiring manager's decision was based on the receptionist's impressions. Remember, the hiring manager and receptionist are in cahoots.

Always walk in the room, and observe first. Inconspicuously scan the room to determine who you would like to meet. Remember, everyone at these networking events is doing the same, so be prepared to make a great first impression.

5. **Approaching People:** When deciding on a person to meet, I always try to approach someone alone or not speaking with anyone. Please walk up to that person, glance at their name tag, and introduce yourself. Use the person's name often without overdoing it. Always present yourself in a pleasant, friendly way, and always smile. Be warm, sincere, and have a sense of humor. Establish an honest rapport upon which you can build a relationship. During your conversation, try to offer information that they may find valuable.

6. **Name Tags:** At some networking events, you may be expected to wear a name tag. If this is the case, remember always to wear your tag on your right side. That is because you use your right hand to shake, and each party's eyesight is automatically directed to the side the tag is on. It merely makes it easier for folks to read your name tag.

7. **Introductions:** Remain courteous to those introducing themselves to you by listening to them. That can help you to remember their names. Shake their hand correctly, and give them good, respectful eye/face contact.

8. **Alcohol:** It is rare, but some networking events serve "light' alcohol at the end of the day. That can be very risky! I believe it could be a trick or trap to get you to drop your guard and reveal your real character. Business etiquette says to avoid alcoholic beverages at networking events or if offered a drink at an interview. Intoxication, slurring your words, alcohol breath, vomiting, and the inability to stand while at a networking event or interview are unacceptable behaviors.

9. **DON'T SMOKE!** Did you know that it cost the average company about $15.000 a year extra to employ smokers? When you combine more sick time, additional health coverage, smoking breaks, and a designated smoking area, the money accumulates quickly. Discrimination against smokers is as high as racial, age, and gender discrimination. Therefore, you must not smell like smoke at any of these events. If you are a smoker, it's ideal to have your last cigarette before you hop in the shower. Then put on your clean smelling clothes, and then attend the event or interview. I'm sorry we live in a world where these discriminations exist. I just want you to be aware of this information because I'm looking out for you.

10. **Don't Lie:** Never misrepresent yourself at an interview or event. The words you speak must always be honest and served with integrity.

11. **Respect & Courtesy:** Treat everyone you meet (including your competition) with respect, dignity, and courtesy. Never engage in any slanderous comments about anyone. Show respect and courtesy towards your competitors.

12. **Be Positive:** Always project a positive attitude. People will always remember your positive enthusiasm. It is also human nature to want to associate with positive people. Negative people are downers and usually not welcomed at networking events.

13. **Business Cards:** Business cards are tricky. If you don't have professional business cards, don't worry about it. Your resume should contain all of the required contact information. However, if you have business cards, the soft skill rule is not to give them out until someone asks you for it. You should only

exchange business cards after you have established rapport with someone. Research indicates that if you randomly hand out business cards, most people will throw them out. However, if you spark a strong interest in the other person and they ask for your card, you significantly increase the chances they will contact you. When receiving a business card from someone, take the time to read it before putting it in your pocket. It demonstrates respect. When you part ways, write notes on the back of their card to remember what you discussed and re-establish rapport after the event. On a different note, business cards will soon be extinct. Today, when people make contact, they quickly connect at the event on LinkedIn or their cell phone.

14. **Follow-Up! Follow-Up! Follow-Up:** Attending a networking event is only the beginning. Now you must begin to develop the relationship. Perhaps you can start by sending them a short email, card, or note, thanking them for the courtesy they offered during the event you attended. If someone gives you a gift, the "ideal" thank you card or note is always handwritten, unless you have terrible handwriting. Of course, you can always send a short-email instead. Also, call them shortly afterward and continue nurturing the relationship. 61% of professionals agree that regular interaction with their professional network can lead to terrific job opportunities. Never stalk people!

15. **It Never Ends:** Networking is an ongoing process; it never ends. However, when you do it consistently and adequately, fantastic job and career opportunities will become available to you.

Chapter 12 Review

1. Live or online networking dramatically increases your chances of landing an interview and getting hired.

2. It's important to know that 80% of in-demand, high-paying jobs never get posted and are only found through networking. In other words, many great jobs are kept secret.

3. Networking should be continuous and fun.

Chapter 13

The Anatomy of a Job Interview

Would you like a "behind the scenes" tour of what to expect at your job interview? If you are experienced in the interview process, you will enjoy this point of view. If you're new to the interview process, this information can eliminate the stress and anxiety, making you more comfortable.

Interview Anatomy Part 1

A typical job posting will attract about 250-300 resumes. The most popular way to submit a resume is through the company's online process. The link should be on the job posting. Once your application and resume are submitted, a human being will rarely read them. The first step is that your resume is filtered through the Applicant Tracking System (ATS). All larger companies utilize this system. The ATS is programmed to pick out keywords or phrases on your resume that best match what they are seeking in a candidate. The ATS saves time, cutting down on the number of resumes a hiring manager needs to review. If your resume does not contain the required keywords, it gets rejected, and they send you a "thanks but no thanks" form letter.

The key to getting past the ATS is to add some of the terminology, jargon, or specifics they used in their job posting into your resume and cover letter. You must customize your resume using language found in the job description. For example, if they are looking to hire a "Customer Relations Expert," use that terminology instead of stating that you are a "Customer Service Representative." If they are looking to hire a "Team Leader," use that terminology instead of saying that you are a "Team Manager." If they are looking to hire someone who is an "Excellent Computer Programmer," use that terminology instead of saying that you are a "Computer Expert."

Interview Anatomy Part 2

A human being will only read your resume if it makes it past the ATS. If it does, the hiring manager will spend an average of six seconds reviewing it. That means you don't have much time to catch their eye. While this is not a book about designing your resume, I would like to offer you some quick tips to help your resume stand out and get noticed.

1. There is **NO SUCH THING** as a perfect resume. However, you do need to be sure yours is neat and orderly. It should not be a long laundry list of your entire career and work history. Also, be sure to check your spelling and grammar.

2. Your resume should be one page or two pages max, **NEVER** longer than that. Also, it should not go back further than ten years. Over 35% of resumes get tossed because they are too long and difficult to read. Be sure your resume discusses your achievements more than your skills. In other words, instead of saying you were a sales rep for ABC Company, say you had a closing rate of 80% for ABC company. Always focus on your achievements. Sell your achievements, not your skills.

3. You must always include a cover letter! Your cover letter should only be about 3/4ths long and borrow terminology and qualifications listed in their job posting without plagiarizing it. Most recruiters and hiring managers **WILL NOT** read your cover letter. However, they do like that you took the time to write one. It shows your professionalism, determination, and commitment. A cover letter helps you to get noticed.

4. Instead of using Times New Roman, pick a contemporary font like Calibri, Arial, Cambria, Palatino, or Verdana—all of which are standard typefaces, so they'll translate just fine between operating systems, but once you choose a font, stick to it.

5. To avoid age discrimination, immediately remove the "Personal Objective" statement and the "Professional References Available Upon Request" statement.

Remember, your resume is a sales tool; therefore, your "personal objective statement" has little value because it focuses on what you want rather than what you can offer to the company. Also, "references available upon request" is a waste of time and space because you're mentioning something that a potential employer expects you're able to provide. Therefore, don't state the obvious. These mistakes make you look out of touch and old.

6. You also look old if you're still using AOL or Hotmail for your email accounts. Over 76% of resumes are discarded because of an unprofessional email address. Therefore, upgrade your email address ASAP. I'd recommend using a generic email provider such as Apple/Microsoft mail, Yahoo Mail, or Gmail. If possible, use your full name in your email so the hiring manager can remember it. And **TRY NOT** to use any numbers in your email address. The hiring manager may misconstrue the numbers to represent your age or birthday, which could "date" you.

7. Make sure your resume is online and posted on LinkedIn. Research states that if you have a comprehensive LinkedIn profile, you have a 71% higher chance of landing an interview than those who do not.

Interview Anatomy Part 3

Now that you've escaped the clutches of the ATS, your resume landed in human hands, and they liked what they read, the hiring manager will now check out your social media pages. If you have a website, include the link at the bottom of your resume. Also, include the link to your LinkedIn page. This will save the hiring manager time, and they will appreciate you for it. Be sure your social media pages do not contain any graphic photos or postings that will cast a dark shadow or incriminate you in any way. Remove anything that has to do with religion, politics, or conspiracy theories. Hiring managers, head-hunters, or recruiters will not schedule you for a phone interview if they do not like your social media content. **CAUTION** – do not send out a resume or apply for a job until you clean up your social media.

Interview Anatomy Part 4

Now that the hiring manager likes your social media content, the next step is to schedule you for a telephone interview. Scheduling your telephone interview is usually set up through email.

There are several things you need to be aware of so you are prepared for the call. Remember, you want to make a great first impression, and it takes only five seconds to do that over the phone.

1. The first thing you need to do is change your voicemail to a professional greeting should you miss the call or they call you earlier than expected. Be sure your diction is clear, and your tone is happy, friendly, and professional. Use the name you used on your Resume/Application. Ask them to please leave a name, number, and message, including the best time to call back. Be sure your voicemail is not full, and check this regularly.

2. **DO NOT** pick up the call if you're dealing with an emergency, a lot of background noise, or limited connectivity. In this situation, the ideal thing is to let the call go to voicemail. Sometimes, when a potential employer calls and leaves a message, they may also follow up with an email. So, check your email regularly, including spam.

3. Get cleaned and dress professionally for the call. The research concludes that if you are doing a phone interview in your PJs, you will not be as resourceful as you would be if you are dressed professionally. Take it as seriously as an in-person interview. Obviously, if it's a Zoom call, you must dress the part.

4. Usually, only one hiring manager will interview you on the call. However, at an in-person interview, there may be several. The only goal of the interview phone call is to try and eliminate you. Why? When it comes to face to face interviews, they only want to commit their time to meet the best of the best.

5. The call can last about fifteen minutes, or longer if they like you. They will ask basic questions such as resume information, availability, travel, your personal life, potential salary expectations, common job interview questions, and possibly a few "oddball" questions. They may also ask if you have any questions.

6. The caller expects you to be focused, without distractions. You should engage in a back and forth dialogue without ever dominating the conversation. Remember to pause, listen, watch your diction, and project a "controlled" enthusiasm. I highly recommend you research the company, read their website, and always keep a cheat sheet with you.

7. **DO NOT** be discouraged if they do not mention the "next" interview to you. This does not mean that they eliminated you or don't like you. It's just not a common practice. They will usually send you an email if they want to schedule a

face to face interview. However, if they're going to set up the next interview, remember to ask for the name of the person who will be interviewing you. Then, look them up on LinkedIn to learn about their background and determine if you have anything in common. You can utilize these commonalities as an ice-breaker when you meet.

Interview Anatomy Part 5

All right! Let's take a look at what has happened to you so far:

- You submitted an application, cover letter, and resume online.
- You included keywords and language from the job posting, and the ATS liked you.
- The ATS passed your approved resume to a living hiring manager; it caught their eye; they read it and liked it.
- The hiring manager then checked you out on social media and liked what they saw.
- The hiring manager then scheduled and conducted a phone interview with you. And of course, they like you even more.
- After comparing you to the other interviewed candidates, they now schedule a face to face interview. Hallelujah!!!!

What Must I Bring to My Interview?

You've worked hard to earn this interview, and you want to set yourself up for success while minimizing failure points. Here is a list of things you should bring to your interview:

1. Bring a professional folder, attache case, or binder & note pad. It is perfectly acceptable for you to jot down a few notes during the interview if necessary.

2. Have at least two pens. Do not ask the receptionist for a pen. Asking to borrow a pen means you showed up unprepared, and they will report it to the hiring manager. If you fail to return the pen, that means you're a thief. Remember, the hiring manager and receptionist are in cahoots.

3. Carry at least five copies of your resume should they ask for extra or more than one person is interviewing you. If you are attending a job fair or networking event, bring at least fifty copies of your resume.

4. Always have directions & contact information in case of an emergency. If you're using google maps and your phone dies, at least you'll have the directions with you.

5. Bring a copy of your references with you in case they ask you for it. You need three professional references, their phone number, email address, number of years you've known them, and their title. You may enter a building and first meet with a security guard in many cases, so remember to always carry your photo ID with you.

6. If you are applying for a job in a creative field, you will need to bring your portfolio.

7. Your folder or briefcase should also include any questions or talking points and a copy of the job posting. As a special homework assignment, please do the following:

> A. A day or two before your interview, visit the company's website, print out a copy of their Vision/Mission Statements, and a copy of their Value Statements. All good companies have these on their website, usually listed under the "About Us" tab.
>
> B. Place these copies and the copy of the job posting directly in front of you. Please read them, and then using a yellow highlighter only, highlight the values you have in common or can most relate to and the parts of the job posting that most excite you.
>
> C. Then, if during the interview, they ask you: *"Why do you think you will do well in this job?" "Why are you the best person for this job?" "What kind of contributions can you make to this company?" "What interests you most about this job?" "Why should we hire you?"*
>
> I want you to take out your highlighted copies and say confidently – *"I'm glad you asked that question. A few days ago, I reviewed your website and came across your compelling vision and mission statements, along with a list of the company's values. I was so impressed with what I read; as you can see, I copied it and highlighted the sections that dovetail with my values. I believe since our values and mission so closely match, I'm confident I would be an excellent fit for your team and bring many benefits to your culture."*

(When you say, *"I'm confident I would be an excellent fit for your team and bring many benefits to your culture."* Be sure you're using your body language and **SUBTLY** nodding your head up and down, indicating "yes." This is known as giving them the "Yes Visual." I highly recommend you review chapter 3 and review the content about body language, and giving someone a "visual.")

I have stacks of emails and personal letters from people all over the country, stating that they answered those questions using that strategy and were hired on the spot. One lady in New Jersey told me it helped her land a $150,000 a year job, and she is thrilled. It's a terrific approach and solid answer because you are using "their own" words from "their own" website, and they can't help but be impressed.

8. If you have a quick snack before your interview, be sure to carry some breath spray and floss with you. Don't use gum or breath mints because you may forget they are in your mouth, and it's disrespectful to chew gum during an interview.

Interview Anatomy Part 6

It's finally time for your interview, and I'd like to combine some soft skills and business etiquette into the following section. Now before you gently knock on the office door ten minutes early, let's do a double-check:

- You have your briefcase or binder.
- You read their website.
- You have your yellow highlighted job posting and their values and mission statement.
- You did not smoke.
- You've dressed appropriately, and you've checked your breath and teeth.
- You have your three references if required.
- You have two pens and five copies of your resume.
- You have a small list of questions or talking points.
- Your cell phone is off.

1. After you knock and enter the reception area, meet and greet the receptionist with a smile, enthusiasm, and a positive mental attitude. Remember, the interview begins the moment you meet the receptionist.

You - *Good Morning! My name is John Eric Jacobsen, and I have an appointment to meet Mrs. Davis regarding the teaching position.*

Receptionist – *Sure, John. I'll let Mrs. Davis know that you are here; please have a seat.*

You – *Thank you so very much.*

If the receptionist asks, *"How was your commute?"* Or, *"How are you dealing with the heat, rain, or snow?"* Always respond with a cheerful *"Great!"* Or, *"No problem at all!"* They may be testing your attitude or positivity factor.

Receptionist – *Mr. Jacobsen, Mrs. Davis, will see you now.*

You – *Thank you so very much; I appreciate your help.*

2. Meet and greet the hiring manager (head-hunter/recruiter) with a smile, enthusiasm, a professional handshake, eye/face contact, and a positive mental attitude.

YOU - *Good Morning, Mrs. Davis! I'm John Eric Jacobsen. It's a pleasure to meet you, and I appreciate your time.* (Subtly give them the "Yes Visual.")

Confidently walk into their office and do not sit down until they invite you to sit. This is basic business etiquette. After they offer you a seat, thank them. If they do not offer you a seat, politely ask, *"With your permission, may I sit?"* And while asking for permission, give them the "Yes Visual." Your body language will send them a subconscious signal to answer "yes," and then they'll ask you to sit. Remember, your body language speaks louder than your mouth. During the interview process, do not:

   *Act desperate or hopeless.

   *Give canned answers to tough questions.

   *Throw your current or former company or manager under the bus.

   *Disclose your family status (or other protected information).

   *Blame others for things in your past.

*Ask about salary and benefits too early.

*If it is a group interview, do not play favorites.

Interview Anatomy Part 7

When your interview is completed, the hiring manager will probably ask if you have any questions. I recommend you have at least three prepared. However, you do not need to ask all three. Use your gut to determine the "temperature" of the hiring manager. Does it feel like they want to talk more, or are they rushing you out the door? Again, have three questions prepared and let your gut guide you. For your consideration, at the end of this chapter, I've listed several questions you might ask at the close of your interview. As I mentioned earlier, it's OK to jot down occasional notes. Shake the hiring manager's hand, and thank them for their time.

You – *I want to thank you so much for meeting with me today and thank you for the courtesy of your time. With your permission, may I ask when you might be making a decision regarding this position?*

Wait for their replay, thank them again for answering that question, and then add:

You – *Also, may I ask for your business card?*

You need to know when they will be making a hiring decision so that you can gauge when they might contact you again. You need their business card so you can send a "thank-you for interviewing me" email. If they don't have a business card, ask the receptionist for the hiring manager's email address as you walk out the door and explain that you want to send a thank-you email. You significantly increase your chances of landing the job if you send a thank you email to the hiring manager. It's a soft skill that must not be overlooked or forgotten. Lastly, be sure to thank the receptionist and wish them a good day.

Interview Anatomy Part 8

CAUTION: I have witnessed hundreds of hiring managers peak out their window to watch a potential candidate depart the company site. Therefore, you must remember **DO NOT** remove your tie or jacket, spit in the grass, pick your nose, or smoke until you are in your car and entirely out of their parking lot or walked totally out of the building view.

"The interview is not over until you can no longer see the building."

You worked very hard to create an excellent first impression, be sure you leave them with a good last impression.

Questions You Can Ask During or at the Close of Your Interview

1. As I read through your website, I noticed that your company values dovetail with my personal values. (Give examples) Is that important to you when adding a new member to your team?

2. What are the personality types that best fit into your group?

3. What makes the most successful employees on your team successful?

4. What is the average length of time an employee remains with the company?

5. How long was the last employee in this position, and where are they now?

6. Where do you see the candidate in this role in two years?

7. In your opinion, what makes this available position exciting?

8. If you were to hire me today, what three goals do I need to reach in the next 90 days, so that you say hiring me was a great idea?

9. If you were to hire me today, what could I do to make your job easier?

Chapter 13 Review

1. Re-read this chapter!

Chapter 14

How to Write a Great "Thank You" Email

I've seen a lot of amazing things in my career. However, nothing amazes and puzzles me more than the 50% of job-seekers who forget to send a thank you email after an interview. Over 25% of head-hunters, hiring managers, or recruiters will quickly eliminate candidates if they do not send a thank you note. Recently a survey revealed that 80% of HR managers consider thank you emails helpful for reaching their final hiring decision.

I'm a big fan of thank you notes. They are an essential ingredient of soft skills, and I highly recommend them. I also believe they should be an integral part of your job search if you use them properly. What does that mean?

Thank You Note Tips

1. To obtain the most significant impact from a thank you note, send yours out within twenty-four hours of your interview. To be more specific, if your interview ended before noon, send the email at 4 pm the same day. If your interview ended after the noon hour, send the email at 9 am the next morning. If the following day is a weekend, wait until Monday to send your email.

2. Check your grammar and spelling before you email it.

3. Be sure your subject line is clear. You can simply write "Thank you for the interview" in the subject line, or something like "Following up on our interview."

4. And most of all, your note must **never** contain any ulterior motives. In other words, after expressing your thanks, don't beg for the job or rehash your skills. A thank you note should **ONLY** be a thank you note. I see these inappropriate actions often, and I feel it's disrespectful to the hiring manager. It reminds me of a salesperson sending a thank you note to a recent customer and then asking for referrals. Simply express your sincere appreciation, and say thank you. It's that simple yet very effective way to be remembered.

Here are a few examples to get you started. You will need to change some of the terminologies to fit your situation and timing, but they are satisfactory templates.

After Interview "Thank You" Note

Hello, Mr. Daniels:

This is just a quick note to thank you for taking the time out of your busy schedule to speak with me today about the fantastic Customer Service position. I sincerely appreciate your consideration.

I certainly look forward to hearing from you once you make your final decision. Please feel free to contact me at any time if further information is needed.

Thank you again for your time and consideration.

Sincerely,

Jessica Jay

856-123-1234

Let's take a Closer Look

1. Remember, if your interview ended before noon, send the email at 4 pm the same day. If your interview ended after the noon hour, send the email at 9 am the next morning. If the following day is a weekend, wait until Monday to send your email.

2. I do not recommend beginning your email with "Good Morning," "Good Afternoon," or "Good evening." Those salutations "date" or "time-stamp" your email, and the receiver will know when you sent it. Worse, if they don't get the chance to read it until late that evening, your "good morning" greeting may serve as a demotivator, thinking that it's too late to read it now.

3. The first line states, "This is just a quick note." Remember, your goal is to get them to read your email, not skim it. When you tell the receiver this will be "quick," it acts as a motivator to read the email in its entirety.

4. Mention the position for which you interviewed.

5. Mention, "you look forward to hearing from them," without any other ulterior motive. Please do not ask or beg for the job, and do not remind them of your skills. A thank you note should ONLY be a thank you note.

Follow Up Notes

I recommend sending your first follow-up note on the third day after they indicated they would make their final decision. If they said they would decide by next Monday, and you don't hear from them. Send this first follow-up on Wednesday. If the third day is a weekend, wait until Monday to send your email. Notice, in this follow-up note, it's OK to ask for the job.

1st Follow-Up Note!

Hello, Barbara:

I hope all is well with you! You mentioned that you might be finalizing your decision for the Regional Manager position on Monday, and I'm eager to hear when you have an update.

As I mentioned, I'd appreciate the opportunity to contribute to your team and work with you. I know I can bring a lot of management experience and passion to the position.

Please let me know if there's anything I can provide to assist you in your decision-making process or any other questions you may have for me.

Thank you again!

Sincerely,

Erica Louise

856-123-1234

2nd Follow-Up!

A second follow-up note is required if they contact you and say they need another week to finalize their decision. Perhaps, they've decided to interview a few more candidates, which is very common. There may be instances where they keep postponing their decision. If this is the case, you should keep sending follow-up emails or making follow-up calls.

Again, I recommend sending your second follow-up note on the third day after they said they would make their final decision. If they indicated they would decide by next Monday, and you don't hear from them. Send this second follow-up on Wednesday. If the third day is a weekend, wait until Monday to send your email. Notice, in this follow-up note, it's OK to ask for the job.

2nd Follow-Up Note!

Hello, Ms.Leonard:

In your last email, you mentioned that you were still interviewing for the Regional Manager Position. I want to reaffirm my enthusiasm for being considered for the role and confidence in my ability to bring more value to your team.

If there is any additional information I can provide to help move the process forward, please let me know.

Thank you again!

Sincerely,

Richard Bertoldo

856-123-1234

Why didn't You Hire Me?

If the hiring manager sends you a form email that they are passing on you and going with another candidate, you may consider sending them a "Why didn't you hire me" email. This kind of email is **not** required, is **not** expected, and is **not** essential. There are only three specific reasons you might consider sending out an email like this:

1. You're super curious as to why they decided to go with another candidate.

2. You honestly want feedback regarding your interview skills.

3. You're DESPERATE to get your foot in the door at that particular company and want to make one last attempt.

I've sent this email out three times in my entire career after receiving rejection letters, and two of those times, they hired me. In both instances, the hiring managers told me the person they initially hired did not work out, and I was their second choice. The "why didn't you hire me" email put me back on their radar, helping me land an impressive training position. Many students in my classes share similar success stories. A student once asked me if I felt bad or embarrassed about being a second choice. My response was, *"Who cares! As long as I got my foot in the door and they accurately spell my name on the check."*

On another note, most of the time, a hiring manager is too busy to respond to this kind of email, or they can't be bothered. Just remember, if you genuinely want to get your foot in the door at that particular company, sending this email can't hurt.

Why didn't You Hire Me Email?

Hello, Ms. Jones:

Thank you so much for interviewing me for the Accounting Position this month. I enjoyed meeting with you and your team. I was, of course, disappointed that I didn't receive a job offer. Therefore, I'm writing to request a favor.

I am working on improving my interviewing skills. I'm also interested in enhancing areas where I may be lacking. With your kind input, I can work on improving those as well. May I ask for your feedback and advice?

1. Is there any advice you might give me to develop my interviewing style?
2. Did you identify any key qualifications for this job that were missing in my background?
3. Do you have any suggestions regarding how I might improve upon my resume or cover letter?
4. Is there anything you thought I did well?

I understand how busy you are, so I appreciate your feedback and your time.

Thank you again!

Sincerely,

Carla Gigante

856-123-1234

Let me reiterate: This kind of email is **not** required, is **not** expected, and is **not** essential. However, if you want to try it as a last-ditch effort, it will not hurt. Who knows? It may help you get your foot in the door.

Chapter 15

Soft Skills and Answering Tough Interview Questions

22 Most Common Interview Questions

Before we begin this critical chapter, let's take a moment to review a few vital points from chapter 3.

During the first 15 seconds of the first impression, the hiring manager, head-hunter, or recruiter make several judgments about you:

55% of the first impression (which is over half) is a "visual impression" based on how you look and your body language, specifically your facial expressions.

38% of the first impression is an "auditory impression" based on the sound of your voice and the way you speak your words.

7% of the first impression focuses on the feelings and attitudes of your words alone.

As you read the above research, it can give you the idea that your words are the least important part of the conversation. It's not true. If words were an insignificant part of communication, we wouldn't need to learn foreign languages to understand each other. Words are important! However, it is essential to remember that **93%** of all face to face communication is non-verbal. You need to know how to answer these all-important interview questions. However, you must remember that your body language and tonality are factors contributing to your answers. You need to effectively communicate on all three channels – Body Language, Tone, and Words.

Therefore, as I share the following tips, strategies, and possible answers with you, please be mindful that what works for me may not work for you. What sounds great coming out of my mouth might not sound right coming out of yours. You will be most successful if you take the following information and make it your own. Don't be a John Eric Jacobsen automaton regurgitating canned answers. Instead, use these tips as a framework incorporating your own life experiences. In this manner, you'll sound more genuine because you're speaking from your soul. Remember, you will have to support all of your answers with examples.

1. Tell me about yourself?

This is the most popular question you will hear at a networking event, telephone, or live interview.

    A. Your answer must be tailored to meet the company's needs.

    B. At best, it's an "elevator pitch" and should not be longer than two minutes.

    C. Do not rehash your resume or discuss your personal life.

    D. Sound passionate and positive.

"Sure! My background is in theatrical arts and communication. This passion led me to teaching and coaching because I'm very at ease in front of small or large groups. I've always enjoyed training and helping people improve the quality of their personal and professional lives. I bring passion to my work because I enjoy it so much. This passion allows me to work with various people on a variety of topics without tiring. My enthusiasm for this type of role will enable me to create and maintain professional relationships at all levels. And during the Covid Pandemic, I spent my time creatively mastering many virtual learning platforms. This allows me to teach at a distance and present powerful webinar programs to your clients in other states."

2. Why did you leave your last job?

    A. *"I reevaluated my career goals and decided I needed to make a change."*

    B. *"I had been with the company for many years, and although I enjoyed it, I felt it was time for a change."*

    C. *"I wanted to take on new responsibilities that this role and company couldn't offer."*

    D. *"I didn't feel the job was challenging me, nor utilizing my skills to the fullest degree."*

E. *"My position was eliminated, and unfortunately, I was laid off."*

If your company fired you, I recommend you immediately tell the truth and come clean. It's not worth lying and getting caught later if they check your references. Worse, if they hire you and in the future, they discover you lied, it's grounds for termination. Remember these 4 Steps:

A. Never badmouth or throw your former employer under the bus.

B. Take responsibility for what happened.

C. Show the hiring manager the lesson you learned.

D. Show the hiring manager the steps you've taken to ensure you never make that mistake in the future.

3. What qualities do you look for in a boss?

The most popular answer is, *"A good leader who can effectively communicate their vision."*

4. Are you willing to work overtime? Nights? Weekends?

"Yes! I'm willing to do anything to help the company reach its goals. With your permission, may I ask what does overtime, nights, and weekends look like in this company?"

Remember, not only is the hiring manager interviewing you, but you are also interviewing them. It will help if you determine how much overtime and how many nights or weekends are required **BEFORE** accepting the position. This answer demonstrates your flexibility as a team player while simultaneously looking out for your interests.

5. Would you be willing to relocate if required?

Sorry! I can't help you with this one. It's too personal, and only you know your confidential circumstances. Just be aware that 33% of Americans who pick up their family and move a great distance for a new job opportunity are laid off or downsized within five years. Sometimes it's just not worth leaving your roots.

6. Why do you think you would do well at this job?

Re-read and review "What Must I Bring to My Interview" # 7 in Chapter 13.

7. What would your previous supervisor say is your strongest point?

When you answer this question, sound enthusiastic and proud. More importantly, try to connect your answer to the skills and qualifications they are searching for in the job posting.

8. What motivates you?

When you answer this question, sound enthusiastic and proud. More importantly, try to connect your answer to the skills and qualifications they are searching for in the job posting. For example, if it's a customer service position, mention that you are motivated by serving and helping people.

9. What are your salary expectations?

Never go to a job interview without an idea of what you want to earn. While employees who remain at the same company can generally expect a 3% annual raise, changing jobs will generally get you a 10% to 20% increase in your salary, so that's an excellent place to start.

> A. To get a general idea of the salary you should request at your new job, add 10% to 20% to your previous salary.
>
> B. Search online for "Simply Hired" and see if the job you're interested in is posted there. This is a terrific job search site because it gives you a general idea of what that job might be paying."
>
> C. Search online for "Glassdoor." Key in your state and the title of the job you're interested in. Glassdoor will give you an average pay scale for that position in your state.
>
> D. Average those numbers together, and you'll be better prepared when it comes to salary negotiations.

"My salary expectations are in line with my experience. If this is the right job for me, I'm sure we can come up with a salary that matches my qualifications. With your permission, may I ask how much money the company has reserved for this position?" (Give them the "Yes Visual.")

10. What are your goals for the next five years?

"My goal for the next five years is to be sitting here with you, looking back at my many achievements and the many benefits I've brought to this company. I want to be recognized for my expertise and as a loyal team member."

11. What kind of person would you refuse to work with?

Be careful with this one. Your answer may define actual team member's personalities or poor work ethic. There may be lazy people on the team if you answer "lazy people." There may be negative people on the team if you answer "negative people." There may be gossips on the team if you answer "gossip." My answer is always, *"A liar."* This is the safest answer because liars are less common than gossips or lazy people. Also, it's very rare to have a manager admit the team is full of liars. Consider it.

12. How well do you work under pressure?

"When I first began my career, I would infrequently get stressed under pressure. Since then, I've learned some powerful coping skills and perfected some stress management strategies. I also taught myself how to use pressure as a tool to keep me motivated and increase my momentum."

13. Tell me about a time that you participated in a team; what was your role?

Once again, I can't help you with this one. You need to prepare a successful example from your past when you participated on a team and confidently share that story. And, while you're at it, here are a few other stories you **MUST** prepare and rehearse before your interview:

> A. Rehearse a story about a time you saved the day for your team or company.

B. A time you learned a valuable lesson from a mistake.

C. A time you had to act without a manager's guidance.

D. A time when you had to deal with a difficult person.

E. A time you had to change plans and succeeded.

F. A time you took the initiative.

G. A time when you helped resolve a dispute between others?

I promise, if you prepare a success story for each of the above examples, you will nail that interview and impress the hiring manager.

14. Do you prefer to work independently or on a team?

"I'm comfortable working both independently and on a team. However, I prefer working on a team because I enjoy sharing ideas and brainstorming with others."

Or

"I'm comfortable working both independently and on a team. However, I prefer working independently because I can formulate my ideas privately and then share those ideas with my team for feedback and brainstorming purposes."

15. What challenges are you looking for in a position?

Be sure your answer includes some terminology and skills mentioned in their job posting.

16. Why are you the best person for the job?

Re-read and review "What Must I Bring to My Interview" # 7 in Chapter 13.

17. What kind of contribution will you make to our company?

Re-read and review "What Must I Bring to My Interview" # 7 in Chapter 13.

18. What interests you most about this job?

Re-read and review "What Must I Bring to My Interview" # 7 in Chapter 13.

19. I believe you may be overqualified for this job.

"Thank you for the compliment; I appreciate it. I don't know if I'm overqualified, but I'm certainly highly qualified. And I never had a manager complain about a task being completed better than expected."

20. What kind of work do you enjoy the most?

Be sure your answer includes some terminology and skills mentioned in their job posting.

21. Why should we hire you?

Re-read and review "What Must I Bring to My Interview" # 7 in Chapter 13.

22. What is your greatest weakness?

There are five essential steps you must utilize when answering this question:

    A. First, mention the weakness without making it sound like you started a civil war. Please don't make it sound worse than it might be.

    B. When answering, change the word "weakness" to "issue." The word "issue" softens the conversation making it sound better than it might actually be.

    C. Mention the steps you're using to fix the issue.

    D. Discuss how you completely corrected the issue or how much of the issue you corrected thus far.

    E. Never say you don't have any weaknesses.

"I don't know if it's a great weakness, but it's certainly an issue I found challenging. As a trainer, I found it embarrassing when I could not remember my seminar attendees' names. If someone's name slipped my mind, I found it challenging to connect and build rapport with them. Then, I purchased a great book about remembering names and faces by Harry Loraine entitled "The Memory Book." I studied the book and began applying it in my classes. I'm proud to say it really helped me. In the past, I was only able to remember about 20% of my

attendee's names. Now I can remember about 80%. I haven't perfected my skill yet, but I'm on my way and feel good about my accomplishment."

Job/Employment Remorse

Did you ever spend a large sum of money on a product or service you fell in love with, only to regret the decision a few days or weeks later? Perhaps it was a car or home. This is known as "buyers remorse." It's an ugly place to be in and a dreadful way to feel.

This same phenomenon happens to about 23% of Americans when they begin a new job or career. It's called "job remorse," and it's strikingly prevalent with people desperate for work who accept the first job offer they receive. It's sad! There are five reasons most people intentionally leave their jobs:

1. They dislike their manager or supervisor. Most people don't quit jobs; they quit their manager.

2. They dislike the working environment or people.

3. They're seeking a greater opportunity for growth and utilization of their talents.

4. They are seeking a better work-life balance.

5. They lost their passion for the job.

I want to place you in a position where you can effectively minimize the experience of job remorse. While receiving a job offer can be the thrill of a lifetime, you need to approach with care. You can't blindly accept an offer or sign a contract until you have some important questions answered. Some of these questions may be answered during your interview, or maybe not. Some of them may apply to you, and some may not. Therefore, use the following list as a guidepost to guarantee you don't experience any negative surprises in your new career or job.

10 Questions to Ask Before Accepting a Job Offer

1. What are the specific working hours?

2. Does the company offer flexible hours?

3. What are your expectations regarding reaching me after hours? I usually respond to emergency email messages and texts, and I check both infrequently on the weekends. Does that work for you?

4. What are the rules or norms for taking time off? How does vacation, personal, and sick time work? What about occasional hours if I need a doctor's appointment or something else?

5. What are your norms for working at home, especially during inclement weather, or I'm not feeling well but not sick enough to take a sick day?

6. Who are my internal clients, and what are the expectations around my interactions with them? How can I communicate my off-hours availability to those folks?

7. Who will be evaluating my performance in this role? What are the evaluation criteria?

8. Tell me about my most important internal clients and other contacts. What do I need to know about working with each of them — their particular requirements, quirks, communication styles, etc.?

9. What do you think will be the most challenging part of the role? What is your advice for tackling that obstacle?

10. Can you please explain the health benefits?

Chapter 15 Review

1. You must communicate effectively on all three channels when answering your interview questions: Body Language, Sound, and Words.

2. Always speak in a confident, enthusiastic tone. Sound happy to be at the interview.

3. It's advantageous if you take a "slight pause" before answering questions to gather your thoughts.

Chapter 16

Commit to Becoming a Life-Long Learner (It's no longer a choice.)

"I'm still learning." Michelangelo age 87

When I was a youngster, I watched television on a twelve-inch black and white screen, my music was on vinyl playing through a mono speaker, and our phone was bolted securely to the wall. To quote Bob Dylan, *"The times they are a-changing."* Today our television screens are at least fifty inches, in 4K color, and flat. We stream our music through 13.2 home theater sound systems while our telephones fit in our pockets and contain all the information available on the internet. It's amazing!

Place a Check Next to Each Statement that Sounds Like You:

1. *"I can't keep up with the new technologies."*
2. *"Information is flowing faster than I can absorb it."*
3. *"I don't know enough."*
4. *"I'm inadequate and not smart enough."*
5. *"I don't know where I fit in."*
6. *"If I lose this job, I'll be unqualified for anything but an entry-level position."*
7. *"I have great ideas, but I feel stupid presenting them; they may laugh at me."*
8. *"I don't speak the lingo anymore."*

Please do not feel incompetent or isolated if you use this kind of self-defeating terminology. It's common amongst the employed and the unemployed. The information age has quickly become the bombardment age, and keeping up can be challenging.

Biology teaches us that the organism with the most amount of flexibility controls that system. The same is true in business. The most valuable employees are the ones with the greatest amount of flexibility to handle the most challenges.

Studies conclude that the perfect strategy for maintaining your flexibility, agility, and ability to pivot is to keep your education current. This does not necessarily mean you need a diploma or letters of degree after your name. Some of the most successful people on Earth did not attend a school or have a formal education. However, this **DOES** mean you must continuously strive to keep yourself sharp and current. You must continuously "re-tool" yourself to remain cutting-edge. Today, you can't just accept a job, settle in, think you're set, and coast. The competition will destroy you overnight.

"I Didn't Have Time!"

I recently surveyed a group of 2500 people who were downsized or let go from their jobs. They were all in agreement that they could not keep up with the fast-paced influx of information and the ever-changing, upgrading technologies. Once again, nothing to be embarrassed about; this is a common occurrence. However, when I inquired why they didn't try to stay afloat by keeping up-to-date with the new information and technology, the standard answer was, *"John, I didn't have time."*

I want to address this "time-issue" and share some of the latest statistics on how the average American spends their time. The moment you see this bigger picture, you may discover you **DO** have enough time to keep yourself educated and re-tooled.

Check these Out!

The average American **works** a combined **ten years** in a lifetime.

Women spend **seventeen years** of their lives trying to **lose weight.**

Women spend nearly **one full year** deciding what to **wear.**

Women spend **eight years** of their life **shopping.** (That's over 1 hour every single day.)

Women spend **two years** doing their **hair.**

The average **man** will spend one year **staring** at women.

Men spend about **three years** of their life **shaving** and doing their **hair.**

You spend **one full year cleaning.**

You spend **three years cooking.**

You spend almost **four years** sitting at a table **eating.** (About 67 minutes a day.)

The total amount of food you **consume** in a lifetime is close to **thirty-five tons.**

You **walk** a total of **110,000 miles.** (That's equivalent to four times around the world.)

Think about it! Somewhere in this colossal mountain of time, we must be able to find a few minutes daily to educate ourselves. Here is some staggering news:

The Sad News

Less than 2% of Americans have a library card.

46% of American adults cannot understand the label on their prescriptions.

50% of U.S. adults are unable to read an 8th-grade level book.

33% of U.S. high school graduates will never read a book after high school.

42% of college students will never read another book after they graduate.

80% of U.S. families did not buy a book this year.

62% who purchase or download a book will never read it.

These statistics are difficult to imagine but make it easier to understand why the bottom of the success ladder is so very crowded.

Rumor has it that the trucking industry and 2-3 million truck drivers will be replaced over the next several years by automatic, self-drive trucks. I don't know if this is true or not. However, I have seen a noticeable uptick in drivers attending my classes. They all have the same goal: to re-tool themselves and be better prepared for an unpredictable future. Focusing on the fact that learning must be a lifelong activity, here are some tips to sharpen your saw, remain flexible, and maintain cutting-edge skills:

1. Attend as many training seminars, conferences, and workshops as possible.

Especially if you apply for a managerial position, it's critical to keep yourself up to date with the latest skills by continually developing your talents. There are thousands of live training opportunities available to you daily throughout our country and online. Please take advantage of them. Most of all, remain open-minded and curious. Never think you, know-it-all. The best way to learn is to check your ego at the door.

2. Attend training as a group to enhance your learning experience.

Research indicates that if you attend training with a friend, co-worker, or your entire team, it dramatically enhances the learning experience. You'll be in a better position to hear each other's questions and insights. You'll be able to witness team members have creative and strategic breakthroughs. More importantly, you can share ideas and concepts more effectively because you all had a shared learning experience. You can also improve your recall of information by teaching another person or group what you've learned—the fastest way to learn is to teach.

3. Begin reading more magazines, websites, periodicals, and books in line with your career.

I mentioned earlier, the average American reads less than one book per year after high school or college. We spend about three hours a day watching television. The average American spends about two years watching television commercials in a lifetime, and 70% of our waking lives are involved in social media. Again, somewhere in this mountain of wasted time, we must be able to find a few minutes daily to improve ourselves by reading and learning.

Did you know that if you devoted one hour a day to reading material in your chosen field, you'd be an authority on that subject in two years? By the third year, you'd be a national expert, and by the fifth year, you'd be an international authority. Wow! Isn't that amazing? If you are in a management position, you must have a goal and strive to be at least as smart and talented as the employees you're leading. The most common complaint I hear from employees is that they think their manager sucks. They also believe they can easily surpass the manager's leadership skills. They're often baffled at why the manager was hired.

4. Listen to training materials in your car or commute time.

Did you know that the average American spends over four years of their life driving their car? In that time, you'll cover enough distance to go to the moon and back three times! Did you know that the average American spends about three months of their life stuck in traffic? That's approximately thirty-eight hours a year!

"Surely we can utilize this time more effectively."

You can magically transform your vehicle into a university on wheels. If you drive 12,000 miles per year, that equals about 500 hours or twelve 40 hour work weeks. That easily translates into one or two college semesters. Use this time wisely by listening to educational materials in your car or commute time.

On another note, the average American spends about two years of their life in the bathroom and ninety-two days in a lifetime physically sitting on the toilet. Wow, no wonder why they call it the "reading room!" Use that time wisely.

5. Listen closely to your team members and notice how much you can learn from each other.

This is synergy at its best! Remember, the first key in servicing external customers is to create an internal culture where you serve each other. Listening and sharing ideas amongst team members is a powerful way to build this kind of culture and creative momentum. Momentum creates power, and that power creates ingenuity.

6. Remain teachable and coachable.

Continually assess your skills and update yourself. Read voraciously. Scan articles and abstracts for brief updates. Join professional societies. Utilize schools, colleges, universities.

7. Get involved with YouTube.

I've read and studied about 1300 books in my career, some of them more than once. Despite that fact, I don't like reading because I was never good at it. Anytime I sat down to read, my mind wandered, or my eyes hurt, or I would get too fidgety. I've also attended or taught thousands of seminars, workshops, and webinars. These are the strategies I use to keep myself sharp. However, a unique educational platform that has ever entered and blessed my life is YouTube. I love YouTube! I can't believe I can sit down in front of my computer any time of the day or night and take courses and seminars for **FREE**. YouTube taught me how to repair my car, install a dishwasher, install a garbage disposal, paint, write, sing, dance, speak publically, and more importantly, perfect my business craft.

YouTube contains unlimited training videos to improve your soft skills and communication style. It has fantastic videos to help you design your resume and cover letter, and the list is endless. Personally, I'd much rather watch a video than sit down to read.

Chapter 16 Review

1. Your success on the job directly correlates to your ability to keep yourself sharp and flexible.

2. The most successful employees use soft skills, flexibility, and agility to climb the corporate ladder.

3. Read or watch educational videos in your spare time.

4. Convert your vehicle into a university on wheels.

5. Remember, your bathroom is a reading room.

6. Teach others what you learn.

Chapter 17

Soft Skill Strategies for Accelerating Your Career

One day a man walked to the top of a large hill to speak to God. The man asked, *"God, what's a million years to you?"* and God answered, *"A minute."*

Then the man asked, *"Well, what's a million dollars to you?"* and God answered, *"A penny."*

Then the man asked, *"God…..can I have a penny?"* and God answered, *"Sure… in a minute."*

The moral of the story is you are not going to get anything handed to you. And in the business world, hard work is not enough. If you want to climb the corporate ladder and accelerate your career, you have to get NOTICED. You need to establish the "Halo Effect" as early in your career as possible. You must brand yourself as a positive, professional, intelligent go-to team member.

I'm a huge fan of the Dale Carnegie Training Courses and his best-selling book, "How to Win Friends and Influence People." I attended dozens of their courses, and when I first moved to Cherry Hill, NJ, I began working for their company. Not only did their strategies accelerate my career, but they also helped me establish my own successful training business.

I'm also a huge fan of a psychological success strategy know as "modeling." In its most direct form, modeling teaches us to observe and learn what successful people are doing and then imitate their success strategies. In other words, do what successful people do, and you will create the same results. As Tony Robbins frequently says, *"Success leaves clues."*

Therefore, in our final chapter, I would like to offer you a great list of the most successful behaviors and habits you must model and embrace to launch your career and finances into the stratosphere. Remember, competence is not enough; you must get noticed.

With over three decades of experience, I can confidently promise you that these strategies will help you establish the halo effect and get you noticed in the most positive ways possible. You've worked hard. Now it's time to step up and claim the rewards and compensation you've earned and deserve.

31 Strategies for Advancing Your Career and Impeccable Workplace Behaviors

1. Communicate and listen well.

2. Encourage others to talk about themselves and be genuinely interested in them.

3. To build rapport, talk in terms of the other person's interests.

4. Ask for more responsibility on the job, but do not let people take advantage of you.

5. Volunteer, but do not let people take advantage of you.

6. Carry yourself professionally in the way you dress and by projecting a healthy personality.

7. Professionally contribute at meetings with creative ideas and smart questions.

8. Learn as much about your company and business as possible.

9. Say "thank you" to anyone in the office who helps you.

10. Position yourself as a leader by getting noticed as being proactive and flexible.

11. Don't be a "fault-finder." Instead, earn a reputation as "solution-oriented."

12. Don't criticize, condemn or complain. If you do complain, always offer a solution.

13. Give honest, sincere appreciation when appropriate.

14. Make other people feel important—and do it sincerely.

15. Show respect for the other person's opinion. Never say, *"You're wrong."*

16. If you are wrong, admit it quickly and emphatically.

17. Never see things worse than they are. Instead, practice seeing things as they could be.

18. Talk about your own mistakes before criticizing others.

19. Call attention to people's mistakes indirectly. Use encouragement. Make the fault seem easy to correct. Always let them "save face."

20. Be generous in your praise.

21. Honor other people's territory.

22. Honor your working hours

23. Keep your personal information to yourself.

24. Be positive and supportive.

25. Always keep an open mind.

26. Be good at follow-through and follow-up.

27. Honor your commitments.

28. Try solving your own problems before asking for help.

29. Be honest and assertive.

30. Speak with tact and diplomacy.

31. Be professional on your last day.

BEST OF LUCK IN ALL YOU DO!
John Eric Jacobsen January 2021

"Soft Skills – Your Key to a Better Job and Higher Pay"

"Ye Olde Office Rules"

Working conditions have changed quite a bit over the past 150 years. Just read over these office regulations for a New Jersey Carriage Manufacturing Firm in 1872:

I. Employees will daily sweep floors and dust all the furniture.

II. Each day, employees will fill lamps, clean chimneys, and trim wicks.

III. Each clerk will bring in a bucket of water and a scuttle of coal for the day's business.

IV. Employees will make their pens carefully. Nibs may be whittled to the individual tastes.

V. The office will open at 7:00 a.m. and close at 8:00 p.m. daily, except on the Sabbath, on which day it remains closed.

VI. Men employees will be given an evening off each week for courting purposes, or two evenings a week if they regularly go to church.

VII. After an employee has passed his hours of labor in the office, he should spend time reading the Bible and other good books.

VIII. Every employee should lay aside from each pay a goodly sum of his earnings for his benefit during his declining years so that he will not become a burden on the charity of others.

IX. Any employee who smokes Spanish cigars, uses liquor in any form or frequents pool and public halls will give good reason to suspect his worth, intentions, integrity, and honesty.

X. The employee who has performed his labors faithfully and without fault for five years and has been thrifty and attentive to his religious duties will be given an increase of 5 cents per day, providing a just return profit from the business permits.

Author Unknown

About the Author

John Eric Jacobsen is the Co-founder and President of Jacobsen Business Seminars, Inc. John has consulted for more than 1,500 companies and addressed more than 1,000,000 people in 5,000 talks and seminars throughout the country. John is recognized as one of America's preeminent, leading authorities in the area of soft-skills training.

As a keynote speaker and seminar leader, he addresses many people each year on Leadership topics, Surviving Change, Workplace Negativity, Customer Service, Stress Management, Emotional Control, Communication Mastery, Time Management, and more.

Also, a practicing Clinical Hypnotherapist, John is the founder and author of the Kids in Trance Program. This unique, beneficial program teaches parents how to use clinical hypnotherapy with their kids/teens for problem-solving and mental development. http://kidsintrance.com/

Some Clients Include

United States Army, United States Marines, United States Department of Chemical Defense, United Defense, The Interlake Steamship Company, Mormac Marine, Pepsi Cola, Alcon Surgical Laboratories, Subaru of America, Lourdes Medical Center, Comcast, Corning Inc., AT&T, Federal Home Loan Bank, GPU Energy, West Virginia University, Ugg Footwear, VCare Technology, Ashley Furniture, Advanced Gastroenterology, Union County College, Brookdale Community College, Mercer County College, Warren Community College, Rutgers University, and Norwest Mortgage.

http://www.JohnEricJacobsen.net/

Other Books By John Eric Jacobsen

Conversations on Customer Service & Sales

Weapons of Mass Instruction

Soft Skills

The Jesus Lecture

The Kids in Trance Program

"Readers are leaders."